FUTURESCAN

Healthcare Trends and Implications 2007–2012

CONTENTS

Introduction: *Futurescan* in Context 2
by Don Seymour

1 Access to Care: Key to a High-Performance Health System 6
by Karen Davis, Ph.D.

2 Baby Boomers and the Health System: "It's the Workforce, Stupid!" 10
by Jeff Goldsmith, Ph.D.

3 Employers: A Focus on Costs, Quality, and Consumer Empowerment 13
by Helen Darling

4 Philanthropy: Rising to the Challenge 17
by William C. McGinly, Ph.D., CAE

5 Physicians: A Stabilizing of the Social Contract with Hospitals 22
by Thomas C. Royer, M.D.

6 Quality and Safety: Competition Becomes a Market Reality 25
by Janet M. Corrigan, Ph.D., and Cara S. Lesser

7 Clinical Technology: Confronting the Technological Imperative 29
by Lawton R. Burns, Ph.D.

8 Information Technology: Moving Toward an Electronic Medical Record 34
by Thomas M. Priselac and Darren Dworkin

INTRODUCTION: *FUTURESCAN* IN CONTEXT
by Don Seymour

"[R]ight around the year 2000, all ten of the flatteners ... started to converge and work together in ways that created a new, flatter, global playing field."

— Thomas L. Friedman, *The World Is Flat*
(page 173)

About the Author

Don Seymour, president of Don Seymour & Associates in Winchester, Massachusetts, has been working as a strategy adviser to hospital boards, chief executive officers, and medical staff leaders since 1979. A frequent presenter on a variety of subjects related to senior leadership, he is on the faculty of the American College of Healthcare Executives and the Governance Institute. Mr. Seymour has spoken to the American Hospital Association, *Fortune* 100 companies, and a variety of other national, state, and regional groups. He has served as executive editor of *Futurescan*™, the Society for Healthcare Strategy and Market Development's annual healthcare trends publication, since 2004. A past president of SHSMD, he received his MBA degree from Cornell University in Ithaca, New York.

Each year *Futurescan* offers pithy insights on a handful of topics relevant to the strategic issues confronting senior leaders—trustees, physicians, and executives—of the nation's hospitals. We ask each author to present his or her assumptions about the future and to identify key implications for the hospital field. Left up to each individual system or hospital is the task of drawing its own conclusions related to transformation, timing, and context.

Transformation

In *The World Is Flat*, Friedman identifies ten transformational forces leading to globalization. Given, quite literally, a world of changes, he identifies those he believes will be most important in transforming the global economy. He points out that although each trend is important in and of itself, it is the confluence of the ten—how they play off and influence one another—that is the essential driver of change.

Similar conclusions can be drawn about the healthcare field. Although many important changes are taking place that will impact provider organizations, the challenge that the senior leaders of every hospital face is to determine which changes will be influential at the margins and which will come together with the potential to truly transform the core business of the hospital.

Most if not all of us grew up in a world in which healthcare was largely supply driven. When new beds were built with Hill-Burton money and new physicians were trained with support from the Health Manpower Act, patients showed up to occupy both the beds and the offices. The Great Society of Lyndon Johnson further contributed to this phenomenon—what most economists would regard as an inverse supply-demand relationship—by "offering" to pay for the healthcare of some of the older and poorer members of the population through Medicare and Medicaid. Yes, patients made choices based on perceptions about quality (e.g., Massachusetts General, the Mayo Clinic, M.D. Anderson, and some others were arguably "the best"), and most urban markets had some "star" physicians in specialties such as heart and breast surgery. But patients did not have much evidence, if any, to support their perceptions.

Propelled, I believe, by nine transformational forces (Figure 1), the world that most of us grew up in is in the early stages of change, transitioning to an economic model that is driven not by

Figure 1. Nine Forces Transforming Healthcare Economics

Demand Side
1. Transparency
2. Pay for performance
3. Utilization
4. Policy

Supply Side
5. Clinical innovation
6. Workforce
7. Competition
8. Physicians

  9. Information Technology

---

the supply (provider) side, but by the demand (patient, family, payer) side. Space does not permit a full discussion of these trends, but a few illustrative comments are in order.

Transparency—that is, the availability of information about quality, price, and customer satisfaction—will enable the shift to the demand side by arming baby boomers and others with the information to make informed decisions. They will be motivated to make these decisions not just in the interest of their health, but also in the interest of their pocketbooks, as a result of high out-of-pocket costs—the least expensive Wal-Mart employee/spouse health plan offers a $38 monthly premium with a $6,000 deductible (Mui and Joyce 2006)— and triple-tax-advantaged health savings accounts. Providers will increasingly be paid for quality rather than quantity, while, on the supply side, physicians and skilled healthcare workers will be tougher and tougher to find.

If these forces, most of which are still in the earliest stages of development, play out as I believe they will, their impact will be profound indeed. The challenge for each senior leadership team is to incorporate the assumptions set forth by the *Futurescan* authors into its trends analyses, to develop its own list of potentially transforming forces, to debate and discuss the trajectory and convergence of those forces, and to define a set of implications for the hospital or system.

Timing

Equally important as the debate about transformation is a discussion about timing. Too often, healthcare leaders fall into the trap of debating transformational forces in terms of their potential impact in the short (annual) or near (three-year) term. As important as these discussions are tactically and operationally, they are literally short-sighted when considering strategy. With few exceptions, such as hospitals in turnaround situations, hospitals should establish strategy with a view to the next seven to ten years (Figure 2). Are any of us this clairvoyant? The answer is "No, but...."

When a hospital recruits a 32-year-old physician fresh out of training, it has invested cash and human capital in an important collaborative endeavor that it hopes will last 30 years or more. Get it wrong, and the hospital, at a minimum, has to start over. Get it wrong, and the hospital may have to live with its mistake for the next three decades. Or, consider this. If the new multimillion-dollar building project turns out to be a mistake, does the hospital get a do-over? Once again, scarce resources will have been allocated for a building that the hospital will have to live with for a lot

Figure 2. Timing and Content of Hospital Planning Documents

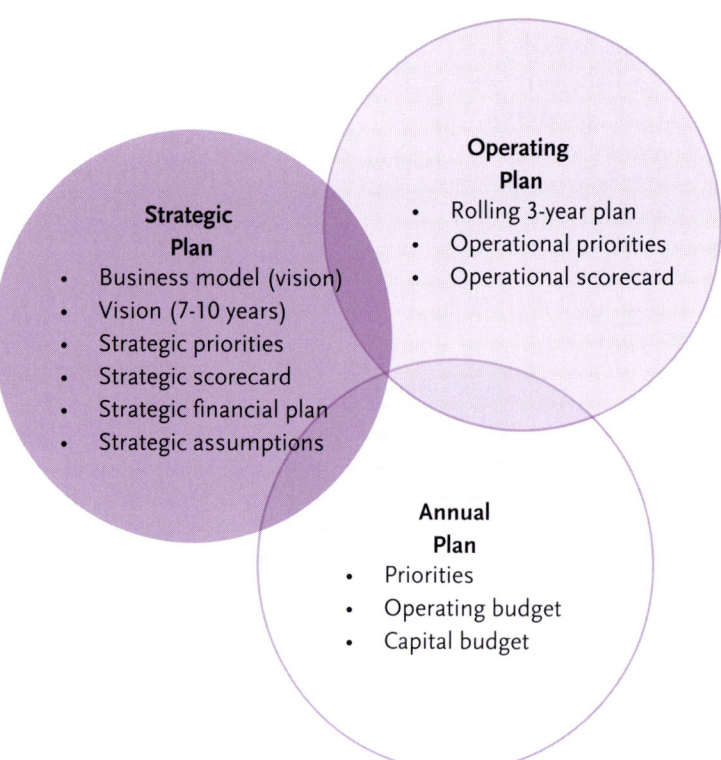

longer than ten years. Finally, many hospitals are rediscovering the need for and potential of philanthropy. Ask a fund-raising expert how long it will take to reengage a neglected community in a philanthropic undertaking to raise tens of millions of dollars. The answer, in my experience, is at least ten years.

Take another example. In 1988, indemnity insurance accounted for over 70 percent of the commercial market. By 2005, its market share was less than 5 percent, having been replaced by HMO, PPO, and POS plans. Hospital leaders debating the future of this trend in the late 1980s or early 1990s would have missed it if they had focused only on the short or near term.

Here is an example from another vantage point. Many hospitals are ramping up their gastric bypass surgery programs, at least in part because of current very favorable payment rates. Other considerations aside (credentialing; retooling doorways; acquiring beds, gurneys, tables, and other equipment; disrupting the OR schedule), this is probably a sound, short-term financial decision. However, providers should ask themselves if they believe the current level of payment will be sustained, or if it will, like the "75 percent rule" for rehabilitation, be ratcheted down over time.

Annual strategic plan updates and assessments are a prudent use of senior leadership time. However, an annual or even three-year strategic plan is a misnomer.

Context

In addition to the issues of transformation and timing, senior leaders should also place *Futurescan* and other trends analyses into the context of their own particular circumstances. Many factors enter into play (Figure 3). If my prognosis is correct, provider economics will tip inexorably toward the demand side over the next ten years. This leads to the overarching conclusion that for any one provider to be all things to all people will become increasingly difficult, and more likely impossible. In a challenge to their full-service mission, many hospitals will be forced to prioritize service offerings, and physicians will be forced to subspecialize. There won't be many general surgeons, but there will be surgeons who subspecialize in breast, colorectal, abdominal, and gastric bypass surgery.

Conclusion

Futurescan 2007 focuses on eight key trend areas that are having an impact on hospitals across the country. We trust you will find the insights useful as you develop your own assumptions about the future of your hospital by:

- Identifying those trends that are truly transformational.
- Assessing your hospital's strategy in a seven- to ten-year time frame.
- Analyzing implications of the trends discussed in *Futurescan* in the context of your organization's particular circumstances.

Figure 3. Organizational Factors Influencing Hospital Strategic Plans

- Service area demographics
- Competitors
- Payment rates
- Service mix
- Medical staff characteristics
- Organizational culture
- Role in teaching and research
- Financial strength
- Age of plant and equipment
- State-of-the-art infrastructure
- Capacity
- Clinical outcomes

References

Friedman, T.L. 2005. *The World Is Flat*. New York: Farrar, Straus and Giroux.

Mui, Y.Q., and A. Joyce. 2006. "Wal-Mart to Shrink Options for New Hires' Health Care." *Washington Post* Sept. 27, D03.

1. ACCESS TO CARE: KEY TO A HIGH-PERFORMANCE HEALTH SYSTEM

by Karen Davis, Ph.D.

About the Author
Karen Davis, Ph.D., is president of The Commonwealth Fund, a national philanthropy engaged in independent research on health and social issues. Dr. Davis has had a distinguished career in public policy and research. The first woman to head a U.S. Public Health Service agency, she served as deputy assistant secretary for health policy in the U.S. Department of Health and Human Services from 1977 to 1980. Before that, she was a senior fellow at the Brookings Institution, a visiting scholar at Harvard University, and an assistant professor of economics at Rice University. She has written extensively on health and social policy issues, including the books *Health and the War on Poverty: A Ten-Year Appraisal* (Brookings Institution Press, 1978) and *National Health Insurance: Benefits, Costs, and Consequences* (Brookings Institution Press, 1976). Dr. Davis received the Baxter Health Services Research Award in 2000 and the AcademyHealth Distinguished Investigator Award in 2006.

Failure to ensure access to care for everyone is the Achilles heel of the U.S. healthcare system. The United States is the only major industrialized country without universal healthcare. Despite our wealth and our commitment of 16 percent of the gross domestic product to healthcare—twice the per capita spending of the typical industrialized nation—almost 47 million Americans do not have health insurance coverage (DeNavas-Walt, Proctor, and Hill 2006). More than a third experience gaps in coverage at some time during the year or are underinsured, without adequate coverage to ensure financial protection (Schoen, Doty, et al. 2005).

The consequences of gaps in health insurance in the market-driven health system are now quite clear. A recent scorecard on the U.S. healthcare system finds that access, quality, and efficiency are intricately linked (Schoen, Davis, et al. 2006). Failure to ensure stable universal participation in the healthcare system leads to avoidable deaths, missed opportunities to prevent disease and complications, lost economic productivity, and high administrative costs. The strains in the system as costs have risen and charitable care is less evenly borne by healthcare providers are becoming increasingly evident. Both the public and healthcare opinion leaders put guaranteeing adequate health insurance for all at the top of the health policy agenda (Commonwealth Fund 2006; Schoen, How, et al. 2006).

Erosion of Comprehensive Health Insurance and Access to Care
Working hard is no guarantee of health insurance in this country. New data released by the U.S. Census Bureau show that more and more Americans—46.6 million in 2005—are uninsured (DeNavas-Walt, Proctor, and Hill 2006). That is an increase of 1.3 million since 2004 and 7 million more than in 2000. Most of the newly uninsured are working adults and their spouses. We are steadily losing affordable coverage for the workforce, with implications for both the personal health and financial well-being of working families as well as for the economy. In an ever more competitive global economy, our national resources must include a healthy workforce able to work, learn, and participate fully.

More and more families are finding it difficult to pay medical bills and struggle with accumulated medical debt. A recent survey found that about half of adults in middle-income families ($35,000 to $50,000 annual income) reported serious problems paying for healthcare and health insurance. In fact, healthcare costs are now stretching budgets, even for those with higher

FUTURESCAN SURVEY RESULTS: Access to Care

How likely is it that the following will be seen on a widespread basis (i.e., in the majority of geographic marketplaces) by **2012**?

	Very Likely (%)	Somewhat Likely (%)	Somewhat Unlikely (%)	Very Unlikely (%)
Consumers will pay more than 20 percent of the total healthcare bill, versus about 13 percent today	49	43	7	1
The continued rise in the number of uninsured and rising out-of-pocket costs for patients will propel the issue of healthcare coverage to the top of the health policy agenda	62	33	4	1
Providers will be under increased pressure to make cost and quality information available to the public	90	9	0.5	0.5
Patients will expect electronic access to their personal health records	42	49	9	0
Medicare, Medicaid, and private insurers will increasingly adopt pay-for-performance methods of payment to reward high-quality, high-efficiency care	55	39	6	1
Providers will pay greater attention to coordinating care across sites and over time	36	53	10	1

incomes. One-third of adults with family incomes between $50,000 and $75,000 a year, and one-fifth with incomes over $75,000, report serious medical bill problems (Schoen, How, et al. 2006).

The Human Toll

This is not just a question of money. On average, people without health insurance die prematurely, and our economy suffers from a less productive workforce (Institute of Medicine 2004). The uninsured often do not have a regular doctor and their care is more fragmented, frequently causing them to undergo the same expensive tests several times—driving up costs for the system and increasing the likelihood of medical errors (Collins et al. 2006a). Alternatively, they end up in the emergency room for conditions that could be treated much more affordably and efficiently by a regular visit to a doctor's office. One bright note is the enactment in 1997 of the State Children's Health Insurance Program, which has expanded public program coverage for low-income children and, in some states, low-income parents. This program has been quite effective at bringing coverage to over 5 million low-income children.

This gain in coverage, however, has been more than offset by the loss of employer coverage. Employers have reacted to rising costs by dropping coverage or cutting benefits. In 2005, the average family premium under employer coverage was almost $11,000 a year. This is a major reason why the percentage of firms providing coverage has dropped from 69 percent to 60 percent since 2000 (Claxton et al. 2005).

In addition, the average deductible in employer plans has increased, adding to the financial burdens on lower- and middle-income Americans. Those with high-deductible health plans of $1,000 per person or more are much more likely to be dissatisfied with their health insurance coverage, face greater financial burdens, and experience difficulties obtaining needed care (Collins et al. 2006b).

With the rise in patient cost sharing, insurance coverage is no longer a guaranteed ticket into the healthcare system. Many of the underinsured report problems obtaining needed care. Forty-four percent of adults with deductibles of $1,000 or more report one of four access problems: they had a medical problem but did not see a doctor, did not fill a prescription, did not see a specialist when needed, or skipped a recommended test, treatment, or follow-up. Forty-one percent of those with high-deductible plans report having problems paying medical bills or have outstanding medical debt (Collins et al. 2006b).

What Needs to be Done?
Healthcare leaders expect that unless there is a major shift in public policy, these trends will worsen. Almost half of survey respondents in the 2006 *Futurescan* national survey think it is very likely that consumers will pay more than 20 percent of the total healthcare bill in 2012, versus about 13 percent today.

Survey respondents conclude that the continued rise in the number of uninsured and rising out-of-pocket costs for patients will propel the issue of healthcare coverage to the top of the health policy agenda. Sixty-two percent think this is very likely, and 33 percent think it is somewhat likely. Only 5 percent think it is either somewhat or very unlikely.

In the absence of action at the state or federal level, uninsured patients will have no alternative but to seek charitable or heavily discounted care. Ninety percent of survey respondents report that it is very likely that providers will be under increased pressure to make cost and quality information available to the public. Patients who are paying may also be more demanding, expecting electronic access to their personal health records (42 percent reporting very likely).

Payers—whether private insurers or public programs—are also likely to become more demanding. More than half of survey respondents think it is very likely that Medicare, Medicaid, and private insurers will increasingly adopt pay-for-performance methods of payment to reward high-quality, high-efficiency care. Such a system has been recently recommended by the Institute of Medicine (Institute of Medicine 2006).

Both patients and payers are expressing increasing concern about the lack of care coordination and the resulting risks of medical error, duplication, and waste. One-third of survey respondents think it is very likely and 53 percent somewhat likely that providers will pay greater attention to coordinating care across sites and over time.

Steps We Can Take Now
Clearly, our healthcare system is failing far too many American families. We need a national solution that ensures that all Americans have affordable, comprehensive health insurance coverage that provides access to the care they need, when they need it. This may sound impossible, but it is not. We can take steps right now to get healthcare coverage for more people while working to cut healthcare costs.

For starters, policymakers can decide not to shift additional costs onto working families through high-deductible health plans and health savings accounts that provide more tax benefits for the wealthy but do little to help the uninsured. Instead, policymakers can close existing insurance coverage gaps by helping employers pool their health insurance buying power, making it easier for disabled people to get coverage under Medicare, allowing older adults to "buy in" to Medicare before they reach age 65, and building on the State Children's Health Insurance Program to cover more low-income parents and single young adults.

Already some states such as Maine, Massachusetts, and Vermont have created new pooling mechanisms and provided subsidies for lower-wage individuals to ensure availability and affordability of coverage for those not covered through employer plans. Massachusetts and Vermont have taken the additional step of requiring some financial contribution from employers who do not provide coverage to their workers. These innovations will bear careful examination to learn from their experiences, and will form a basis for shaping national policy to address this increasingly urgent problem.

Implications for Hospital Leaders
Charity care and bad debt. The deterioration of health insurance coverage and access to care will put greater pressure on hospitals to provide charitable care to the uninsured and low-income insured patients with high deductibles and limited benefits. Bad debt is likely to increase as patients are unable to meet their share of out-of-pocket costs.

Transparency. Transparency and public information—not just on hospital prices, but also on quality of care and the total cost of care over an episode of illness—will increasingly be demanded by patients, private insurers, state governments, and the Medicare program (Collins and Davis 2006). Questions will be raised about the wide variations in cost and quality, with no systematic relationship between higher cost and higher quality.

Health system efficiency. Hospital executives need to be leaders in identifying ways of improving health system efficiency. We know that better care is more cost-effective care. We can encourage savings by investing in tools that improve care for patients with chronic and long-term-care needs, particularly as they transition out of the hospital to home, nursing home, or other settings. Better coordination of care and transitional care as patients move across sites of care and are cared for by multiple providers is essential to improving quality, patient safety, and efficiency.

Adoption of electronic medical records and interoperable health information systems are essential to ensuring that information is shared across all providers involved in the care of a patient. With these types of investments, we can build a new, stronger, and higher-performing health system.

Universal coverage. Hospital leaders should also be in the forefront of calling for universal coverage, with adequate benefits to ensure access to care and protect patients from financial hardship. Nonprofit institutions should define and commit to obligations to serve the uninsured and their communities. They should work with local coalitions to improve access to care, and to seek pragmatic solutions with fair sharing of financial responsibility.

We should not tolerate the fact that millions of people work hard every day, but could lose everything in an instant if they have just one medical emergency. The United States is the only country in the industrialized world that fails to ensure that all of its citizens have health insurance. We can do better. It is time for a comprehensive, national response that makes the U.S. healthcare system truly the best in the world.

References

Claxton, G., J. Gabel, I. Gil, J. Pickreign, H. Whitmore, B. Finder, S. Rouhani, S. Hawkins, and D. Rowland. 2005. "What High-Deductible Health Plans Look Like: Findings from a National Survey of Employers." *Health Affairs Web Exclusive* [Online article; created 9/14/06; retrieved 9/14/06.] http://content.healthaffairs.org/cgi/content/abstract/hlthaff.w5.434v1

Collins, S.R., and K. Davis. 2006. *Transparency in Health Care: The Time Has Come.* New York: The Commonwealth Fund.

Collins, S.R., K. Davis, M.M. Doty, J.L. Kriss, and A.L. Holmgren. 2006a. *Gaps in Health Insurance: An All-American Problem.* New York: The Commonwealth Fund.

———. 2006b. *Squeezed: Why Rising Exposure to Health Care Costs Threatens the Health and Financial Well-Being of American Families.* New York: The Commonwealth Fund.

The Commonwealth Fund. 2006. *The Commonwealth Fund Health Care Opinion Leaders Survey: Assessing Congress's Policy Priorities.* New York: The Commonwealth Fund.

DeNavas-Walt, C., B.D. Proctor, and C.H. Hill. 2006. *Income, Poverty, and Health Insurance Coverage in the United States: 2005.* Washington, DC: U.S. Government Printing Office.

Institute of Medicine. 2004. *Insuring America's Health: Principles and Recommendations.* Washington, DC: National Academies Press.

———. 2006. *Rewarding Provider Performance: Aligning Incentives in Medicare.* Washington, DC: National Academies Press.

Schoen, C., K. Davis, S.K.H. How, and S.C. Schoenbaum. 2006. "U.S. Health System Performance: A National Scorecard." *Health Affairs* Web Exclusive [Online article; created 9/20/06; retrieved 9/20/06.] http://content.healthaffairs.org/cgi/content/abstract/hlthaff.25.w457

Schoen, C., M.M. Doty, S.R. Collins, and A.L. Holmgren. 2005. "Insured but Not Protected: How Many Adults Are Underinsured?" *Health Affairs* Web Exclusive [Online article; created 6/14/06; retrieved 9/12/06.] http://content.healthaffairs.org/cgi/content/abstract/hlthaff.w5.289v1

Schoen, C., S.K.H. How, I. Weinbaum, J.E. Craig, Jr., and K. Davis. 2006. *Public Views on Shaping the Future of the U.S. Health Care System.* New York: The Commonwealth Fund.

2. BABY BOOMERS AND THE HEALTH SYSTEM: "IT'S THE WORKFORCE, STUPID!"

by Jeff Goldsmith, Ph.D.

About the Author
Jeff Goldsmith, Ph.D., is president of Health Futures, Inc., which specializes in forecasting future trends in healthcare technology, delivery, and financing. He also lectures in the M.B.A. program at the Wharton School of the University of Pennsylvania in Philadelphia. His interests include biotechnology and information technology, international health systems, and the future of health services. Dr. Goldsmith is a director of Essent Healthcare, a privately held, investor-owned hospital company, and he advises small technology firms on strategy. He lives at Ricochet Farm in Charlottesville, Virginia.

Baby boomers represent more than one-fourth of the U.S. population, so tracking their movements really should not be all that difficult. Yet this notoriously contrary generation has already faked out the health system. Preparing for the boomers, and assisted by what J.D. Kleinke has called the "twaddle echo factor" (a chorus of groupthink emanating from industry think tanks and "experts") (Kleinke 2001), hospitals are in the process of adding thousands of new beds for the baby boom—capacity that may not be needed in some slowly growing communities for 10 or 15 more years.

Hospitals have read the demand side of the baby boomers wrong; it is not going to arrive in a phalanx of wheelchairs. Baby boomers currently range in age from 40 to 60. (I defy the reader to find a single boomer who thinks of himself or herself as elderly!) Pretending to be 35 will continue for some time to be the main driver of healthcare demand for this population. This drive ignited the explosive demand growth in sports medicine, cosmetic surgery, and diagnostic procedures such as colonoscopies that began during the 1990s. Because many hospitals did not view supporting these services as their core business, much of it escaped into "physician space" across the street.

Despite the wide prevalence of obesity, baby boomers as a generation are healthier than their parents or grandparents, and are likely to continue or even accelerate the 25-year-long trend of declining morbidity among people over age 65, which Kenneth Manton and others have documented (Manton and Gu 2001). Many boomers will be healthier at age 85 than their grandparents were at 65, and, as a result, will remain in the labor force far longer.

At the same time, technology continues to reshape the demand for hospital care. Within the decade, most cardiac, cancer, and GI diagnoses will be made by enhanced imaging technologies. Major joint replacement, spinal fusion, and a significant fraction of heart care will rarely require more than an overnight hospital stay. There will be far fewer strokes and heart attacks, thanks to the wide usage of beta blockers, statin drugs, and over-the-counter anti-inflammatories. Inpatient services will become predominantly ER-driven, linked to acute infections and accidents.

A Workforce Tsunami
While they wait for years for baby boom health services demand to crest, however, hospitals are going to be experiencing a human resource crisis of unprecedented magnitude. As those who live near the ocean realize, the first thing that happens in a tsunami is that the water recedes a long way. To extend our metaphor, when the water recedes, a good chunk of today's healthcare workforce will be carried out with it.

The current U.S. healthcare system is powered by baby boomers.

Most baby boom caregivers will have moved out of direct care provision before the wave of boomer-driven healthcare demand arrives on hospital doorsteps. How the health system copes with the temporal mismatch between health services demand and supply of professionals, technicians, and managers from this generation will determine not only its future economic health, but also, and more crucially, whether it can meet the demands of an aging population when they do arrive.

The average age of registered nurses in the United States is 47 (U.S. HHS 2006). Some 38 percent of physicians are over 50 (Merritt, Hawkins and Associates 2004). The entire senior management cadre of most hospitals and health systems are older boomers. Though their retirement plans are difficult to pin down and may depend on the fickle stock market's performance, baby boom caregivers and managers are already looking for less stressful work than manning hospital ORs, ICUs, and ERs and being on call 24 hours a day.

Healthcare provision is not uniquely vulnerable to the generational transition. The U.S. Department of Labor expects 10 million more jobs than workers by 2010, with the shortage tilted toward the skilled positions (U.S. Department of Labor 2005–2006). School districts are vulnerable to baby boom retirement, as is the federal civil service system, particularly high-stress jobs such as air traffic controller.

The looming talent shortage will surprise hospital management, who have been conditioned to think of workforce shortages as cyclical. This human resources crisis is not cyclical, but rather is due to secular changes in workforce composition. Incremental productivity improvements will not be sufficient to close the gap. Moreover, simply throwing dollars at the problem, through recruitment bonuses and large pay raises, will run up against Medicare and private insurance payment limits, damaging hospital financial performance.

Implications for Hospital Leaders

Although human resource policy has not been viewed traditionally as a major strategic issue, the issue is rapidly becoming strategic, and will require a strategic response and appropriate focus by senior managements and boards.

Increased focus on retention. Retention, not recruitment, of skilled workers becomes the central issue. Today's healthcare management grew up in an era of plentiful supply of health professionals and technicians. The huge surge of baby boomers into the workforce lulled management into a "spare parts" mindset, where workers who left could be easily replaced. High vacancy rates in clinical services have led to reliance on mandatory overtime, temporary staffing agencies, and overseas recruitment—which has the unfortunate effect of removing skilled workers from nations with far more pressing health needs than our own—rather than a searching examination of the burn rate of experienced workers.

Because most hospital accounting systems have not treated human resources as a capital expense, the high cost of turnover is not fully appreciated by senior management. The cost of replacing an experienced OR or ICU nurse, including recruitment, training, and the productivity decrement as newly hired persons master the hospital's information technology (IT) systems and protocols of care, can easily run into the low six figures per nurse (Atencio, Cohen, and Gorenberg 2003).

Job redesign for older workers. Slowing the exodus of boomers from the healthcare workforce will require redesigning work roles to better integrate work with leisure and family obligations. Older workers will be seeking to work less than full time, or to work what seem today to be odd work schedules—six months on and six months off, for example—while retaining health benefits and pension coverage. These accommodations seem like a small price for hospitals to pay to retain these workers' knowledge and commitment.

Older workers will also be asking for the opportunity to learn new skills or even to return to school and can be assisted in doing this by a creative sabbatical policy. Finally, for workers in their sixties and seventies, new work roles similar to emeritus professorships in universities, as well as mentor and project consulting roles (again, with access to benefits where needed), will help facilitate both intellectual growth and the transmittal of important cultural knowledge to younger workers.

Real clinical transformation. Healthcare IT is not just about improved efficiency and error reduction, it is also about redesigning jobs to reduce stress and turnover. Hospitals are in the midst of an historic (and expensive) process: replacing costly and inefficient paper- and telephone-based care management systems with modern, digital clinical software. All too often, however, the essential redesign of clinical roles and relationships is being neglected. Vendors have encouraged hospital managements and boards to believe that "clinical transformation" comes in the box when they buy an enterprise IT system.

Clinical transformation does not come "in the box." This essential and difficult task should precede vendor selection and frame precisely what you ask the vendor to do. This often-neglected task is unambiguously the responsibility of hospital management. By eliminating repetitive clerical tasks and improving scheduling and documentation processes, the redesign of clinical work flow, assisted by intelligent clinical IT, can maximize scarce professional time spent in direct patient care. In turn, this will increase clinical workforce morale and commitment and reduce costly turnover.

Virtual clinical care. Healthcare IT will enable continuous patient monitoring by telepresence technology. The ability to coordinate nursing and physician care will also dramatically improve with the advent of clinical software that enables remote monitoring and management of patients. Seen first with so-called nighthawk radiology, the advent of broadband has enabled clinicians to evaluate, asynchronously and remotely, streams of digital clinical information, and use that information to guide the care process.

Combining live audio and video feeds, an electronic patient record, and clinical decision support, telepresence monitoring of patients by physicians is being rapidly adopted in hospital ICUs. Remote monitoring will spread to other parts of the hospital that care for unstable but not acutely ill patients (cardiac telemetry, 23-hour observation units in ERs, perioperative monitoring of surgical patients), dramatically improving both quality of care and clinical worker productivity. The clinical team will become increasingly virtual, enabling a surprising number of caregivers to work from home. Vital clinical care decisions will not have to wait for physicians to answer their beepers or commute into the hospital, reducing stress both on the physicians involved and on the onsite care team.

Dramatic improvements in clinical workforce productivity will be required for hospitals to weather the workforce transition that has already begun. The era of plentiful clinical and technical workers in the American healthcare system is at an end.

References

Atencio, B.L., J. Cohen, and B. Gorenberg. 2003. "Nurse Retention: Is It Worth It?" *Nursing Economics* 21 (6): 262–68.

Kleinke, J.D. 2001. *Oxymorons: The Myth of a U.S. Healthcare System.* San Francisco: Jossey-Bass, 11.

Manton, K.G., and X. Gu. 2001. "Changes in Prevalence of Chronic Disability in the United States Black and Non-Black Population Above Age 65 from 1982–1999." *Proceedings of the National Academy of Science* (US) 98 (11): 6354–59.

Merritt, Hawkins and Associates. 2004. *2004 Survey of Physicians 50 to 65 Years Old.* [Online information; retrieved 10/7/06.] www.merritthawkins.com

U.S. Department of Health and Human Services, Health Resources and Services Administration, Bureau of Health Professions. 2006. *Preliminary Findings: 2004 National Sample Survey of Registered Nurses.* [Online information; retrieved 10/7/06.] http://bhpr.hrsa.gov/healthworkforce/reports/rnpopulation/preliminaryfindings.htm

U.S. Department of Labor, Bureau of Labor Statistics. 2005–2006. *Occupational Outlook Quarterly.* [Online information; retrieved 10/6/06]. www.bls.gov/opub/ooq/2005/winter/art05.pdf

3. EMPLOYERS: A FOCUS ON COSTS, QUALITY, AND CONSUMER EMPOWERMENT

by Helen Darling

About the Author

Helen Darling is president of the National Business Group on Health (formerly, Washington Business Group on Health), a national, nonprofit membership organization devoted exclusively to providing practical solutions to its large-employer members' health benefit problems and speaking for large employers on national health policy issues. Its 250 members purchase health and disability benefits for more than 50 million employees, retirees, and dependents. In 2003, 2004, 2005, and 2006, Ms. Darling was named one of the 100 Most Powerful People in Healthcare by *Modern Healthcare* magazine. Previously, she directed health benefits at Xerox Corporation, was staff in the U.S. Senate, and served as study director at the Institute of Medicine. She serves on the Committee on Performance Measurement of the National Committee for Quality Assurance, which she cochaired for ten years; the Medical Advisory Panel of the Blue Cross Blue Shield Association's Technology Evaluation Center; the Institute of Medicine's Roundtable on Evidence-Based Medicine; and the board of the VHA Health Foundation.

The costs of the U.S. healthcare system are increasing annually at at least twice the rate of overall inflation, and evidence abounds that there is no end in sight. Healthcare already consumes over 16 percent of the gross domestic product, marching inexorably toward 20 percent in 2015 (Borger et al. 2006). An epidemic of obesity will drive spending even higher and could swamp the health system in ways we are just beginning to see. Saddled with high healthcare costs, our economy overall and legacy companies in particular are less and less able to compete globally.

However, employers are concerned not only about how expensive the system is; after all, the United States is a rich country whose residents spend money on many goods and services that provide less real value than healthcare. Employers also are concerned about serious problems of patient safety and quality. The United States has the highest annual healthcare costs in the world—twice the average of other advanced countries with high standards of living (Anderson et al. 2005)—yet nearly half the care we receive is not of the highest quality, that is, reflecting evidence-based medicine and practices agreed on by professional organizations (McGlynn et al. 2003; Asch et al. 2006). Ironically, some geographic areas where we see the most healthcare services, including a great deal of specialty care, have some of the worst outcomes, according to many years of data reported in peer-reviewed journals (Wennberg, Fisher, and Skinner 2002).

In addition, far too often patients are harmed by unsafe care and avoidable medical errors. In short, employers are very concerned that our $2 trillion healthcare industry has hundreds of billions of dollars of ineffective services and waste larded in it.

Consumer Cost Sharing

Increased cost sharing is one of the most common actions that employers have taken to control costs and give employees and their dependents a financial stake in healthcare decisions. Respondents to the *Futurescan* survey agreed almost unanimously (98 percent) that employers will continue down this path. Seventy percent of respondents said it was very likely that employers will continue to use a number of cost-control methods to control utilization or at least make certain that employees are paying the difference if lower-cost alternatives, such as mail-order drugs, are available.

FUTURESCAN SURVEY RESULTS: Employers

How likely is it that the following will be seen on a widespread basis (i.e., in the majority of geographic marketplaces) by *2012?*

	Very Likely (%)	Somewhat Likely (%)	Somewhat Unlikely (%)	Very Unlikely (%)
The cost of health benefits for employees will continue to grow at 5 to 10 percent per year	59	37	4	0
Employers will increase employee cost sharing for healthcare	80	18	2	0
Employers will adopt more cost controls, such as mandatory use of mail-order pharmacies and prior authorization for very expensive technology, imaging, and prescription drugs	70	27	3	0
As the cost of health benefits approaches the pay of the lowest-wage employees, employers will give such employees a higher subsidy for healthcare benefits or allow them to choose a less comprehensive, more restrictive plan	26	55	17	2
Employers will give employees with healthy lifestyles (e.g., those of average or below-average weight or nonsmokers) a discount on their health and disability premiums to partially compensate them for their lower healthcare costs	33	47	18	2
Consumer-directed health plans (using some form of health spending account) will become the dominant method of private health insurance	13	46	34	7
By 2012, less than half of all employers will offer health insurance to their workers (currently, about 60 percent of employers offer health insurance)	23	48	26	3

Employers are likely to continue to provide a subsidy that will allow employees to get the care they want, with the mix of cost sharing and plan design they choose. For example, some employees prefer to pay higher premiums up front and have less cost sharing at the point of service. Others feel that the most cost-effective package for them is less out of the paycheck but more at the point of care. Most employers, especially large ones, will continue to provide coverage and to pick plans that offer superior consumer tools; access to high-quality, efficient networks; evidence to support patient decision making; and outstanding service.

Cost sharing is already a significant burden on low-wage employees, and it will get much worse as costs increase if employers maintain the current cost-sharing formula (employers 80 percent/employees 20 percent). Eighty-one percent of the *Futurescan* survey panel thought it was very likely or somewhat likely that employers would help low-wage employees by giving them a higher subsidy or offering them less expensive, more restrictive plans.

Consumer-Directed Care

Employers increasingly believe that new health plans, such as consumer-directed health plans, can be an antidote to consumers with unlimited wants, including those who seek medical solutions to poor lifestyle choices. We already see movement to consumer-directed healthcare, where the consumer is in charge of his or her own health and health-services-seeking behavior.

The change has not been rapid, but it has been steady, and, frankly, even employers who are not convinced that high deductible plans are the answer do not see many alternatives. Fifty-nine percent of the *Futurescan* survey panel thought it was very likely or somewhat likely that consumer-directed health plans will be the dominant form of private health insurance by 2012.

Consumerism and consumer-directed healthcare may be best suited to the field's noticeable movement toward personalized medicine, where patients and physicians make decisions that require detailed consideration of each patient's needs and circumstances. Top-down financing and management systems may be even less effective in a world of personalized medicine than they were in the managed care era.

Employers recognize that consumers need much better information, decision-support tools, and lots of assistance navigating the care system during the transition to consumer-directed healthcare. Still, given the technological changes ahead and the number of health problems that are driven by individual choices, it will become increasingly clear that employers will not pay for whatever services the consumer wants.

Employer Provision of Benefits

Even though the provision of health benefits through the workplace is an historical accident and has many flaws, it is likely to remain the norm in the United States for at least the next five years, for several reasons. Health benefits are seen as an essential, competitive benefit for the workforce, so few employers of any size would consider not providing them. Even if many employers wanted to offer alternatives, finding and reaching political agreement on those alternatives—so that workers are not left in the lurch—will be a lot harder and take much longer than most people appreciate.

The *Futurescan* survey panel was not so optimistic. Twenty-three percent of survey respondents thought it very likely that fewer than half of all employers would offer health insurance by 2012. Another 48 percent thought that that scenario was somewhat likely. In the author's view, medium- and large-sized employers are likely to continue to provide health coverage. If problems are severe enough, these employers will provide some benefit until there is a solution that would replace the coverage they provide. Those employers that do not provide coverage today tend to be much smaller, and some are very low-margin businesses.

However, if the trend toward consumer-directed healthcare and higher cost sharing across all kinds of plans does not bring costs more into line with the economy's ability to support them, then government financing (with an employer tax, undoubtedly) may look more attractive to all stakeholders. Whatever changes occur, one thing is certain: employees, retirees, and their dependents will be spending more of their own money on effective services, and a lot more of their own money—perhaps 100 percent of the bill—on services deemed to be ineffective or not evidence based. The transition will be rocky, and no stakeholder will be happy.

Consumer Empowerment

Employers will continue to support initiatives aimed at empowering consumers. This is one of the reasons employers are pushing providers, insurers, and government officials to make cost and quality information available to the public.

Leading employers believe that employees and their dependents should have portable personal health records (PHRs) into which electronic systems of doctors and hospitals can put information so that patients and all providers can have essential information accessible to them at all times. The most sophisticated employers are already working with vendors to provide PHRs to their employees and dependents.

A majority of large employers also are already encouraging their employees and dependents to change their behavior to improve their health. Large employers, which tend to lead the way, are rewarding plan participants for making healthful lifestyle choices, such as taking a health risk appraisal, not smoking, being more active, or participating in a weight control program. Eighty percent of *Futurescan* panel respondents agreed that employers are very likely or somewhat likely to subsidize or reward employees for not smoking or maintaining healthy weights.

Implications for Hospital Leaders

Cost control. Hospital executives will want to demonstrate that they are instituting much more effective cost controls, avoiding duplication of services at the community level, eliminating waste, and closing ineffective services. In some communities, the healthcare capacity is larger than the community can support financially or than the population requires. Unless the community has a booming population, the financial outlook is not going to change. In fact, times will only get tougher, with growing numbers of obese patients, an aging hospital workforce, and an aging patient load.

Although closing services or eliminating programs—even those that are not in great demand or operating at a high level of efficiency—is very hard, it is a battle worth fighting. Now is the time for hospital leaders to identify the most robust services and focus on making them the best performers, operating at the most efficient and effective levels and promoting the organization's excellence.

Patient safety/quality. Increasingly, employers and consumers will want to know which hospitals are committed to having a culture of safety and which hospitals have a board of trustees and an executive leadership team publicly on the record as leading the fight to ensure the safest care. There has to be a sharp reduction in the number of avoidable medical mistakes, especially the most egregious ones, and the public will also insist that the rate of healthcare-acquired infections be lowered.

Hospital executives and trustees can actively participate in the Surgical Care Improvement Project (SCIP) and the initiatives of the 100,000 Lives Campaign. They should publicize their commitment and achievements. More employers and groups like the Consumers Union, with its healthcare-acquired infection campaign, will distribute communications to help the average person understand the importance of being admitted to a hospital that promotes quality, safety, and excellence.

Hospitals will want to have verifiable data to back up their claims, and they will need to ensure confidentiality and a trustworthy process to encourage providers to report adverse events and near misses. At the same time, the public will want assurance that methods to ensure accurate reporting do not become ways for providers to avoid effecting the kind of significant change needed to ensure patient safety and quality.

Empowering consumers through IT. Hospital leadership and physicians will find it harder and more expensive to report required data without new health IT. Hospitals have to make the investments of time, talent, and capital to compete. Transparency is the norm in all parts of society, and it will be central to most healthcare transactions. Employers, other payers, and consumers will want performance data on hospitals and on physicians, at least on an aggregated basis.

At the same time, the healthcare system and the needs of individual patients are so complex and so variable that consumers and patients must have a central role in all healthcare decisions. To be effective decision makers, they need help.

Healthcare leaders need to be ready for consumers who want to access or receive their own medical records electronically so they can update their PHRs. Almost everyone will have one. Consumers will want PHRs to include data from multiple providers and from their previous tests and treatments to ensure the best and safest care in the hospital or ambulatory surgery center.

Consumers will want information about personalized medicine, how they are affected, and what treatment options are most appropriate for them. They will also need *trusted* advisers to help them navigate the health system. For now, employers will be working with health plans and vendors to help employees and dependents cope with the clinical issues.

References

Anderson, G.F., P.S. Hussey, B.K. Frogner, and H.R. Waters. 2005. "Health Spending in the United States and the Rest of the Industrialized World." *Health Affairs* 24 (4): 903–14.

Asch, S.M., E.A. Kerr, J. Keesey, J.L. Adams, C.M. Setodji, S. Malik, and E.A. McGlynn. 2006. "Who Is at Greatest Risk for Receiving Poor-Quality Health Care?" *New England Journal of Medicine* 354 (11): 1147–56.

Borger, C., S. Smith, C. Truffer, S. Keehan, A. Sisko, J. Poisal, and M.K. Clemens. 2006. "Health Spending Projections Through 2015: Changes on the Horizon." *Health Affairs* Web Exclusive [Online article; created 2/22/06; retrieved 10/23/06.] http://content.healthaffairs.org/cgi/content/abstract/25/2/w61

McGlynn, E.A., S.M. Asch, J. Adams, J. Keesey, J. Hicks, A. DeCristofaro, and E.A. Kerr. 2003. "The Quality of Health Care Delivered to Adults in the United States." *New England Journal of Medicine* 348 (26): 2635–45.

Wennberg, J., E.S. Fisher, and J.S. Skinner. 2002. "Geography and the Debate Over Medicare Reform." *Health Affairs* Web Exclusive [Online article; created 2/13/06; retrieved 10/6/06.] http://content.healthaffairs.org/cgi/content/abstract/hlthaff.w2.96

4. PHILANTHROPY: RISING TO THE CHALLENGE

by William C. McGinly, Ph.D., CAE

Healthcare philanthropy is undergoing significant change as the healthcare field faces two defining challenges: the increasing reliance of hospitals on philanthropy to address capital shortfalls, and the heightened scrutiny nonprofit hospitals are encountering regarding their tax-exempt status. Hospital operating margins are declining, the need for capital improvements is on the rise, and the financial realities and community benefit of nonprofit hospitals are increasingly misunderstood by local communities, the press, and politicians. To survive in this environment, successful development officers, chief executive officers (CEOs), and chief financial officers (CFOs) are redefining the role of philanthropy in the hospital-foundation relationship. They are viewing philanthropy as less of an art and more of a science.

A Growing Reliance on Philanthropy

After a relatively flat period of capital spending in which many hospitals underinvested in their infrastructure, capital expenditures are expected to increase substantially in the next five years (Figure 4). Hospitals will need to address deteriorating facilities

About the Author
William C. McGinly, Ph.D., CAE, is president and chief executive officer of the Association for Healthcare Philanthropy (AHP), an organization representing more than 4,000 hospital and medical center executives devoted to fund-raising, public relations, and marketing for nonprofit healthcare providers. He also heads the AHP Foundation and the Hospital Development and Educational Fund of Canada, which conduct annual giving programs and major capital campaigns for the profession. Dr. McGinly currently serves on the boards of directors of the Center on Philanthropy at Indiana University in Indianapolis; eTapestry, a web-based fund-raising software company; and the e-Philanthropy Foundation, an organization dedicated to enhancing online giving. He also is past chairman of the Greater Washington Society of Association Executives, an I/D/E/A/ Fellow, an active member of the American Society of Association Executives, and a Certified Association Executive (CAE). He received his doctorate in administration from American University in Washington.

Acknowledgment
Appreciation is expressed to Catherine Gahres, communications manager, Association for Healthcare Philanthropy, for her assistance in preparing this essay.

Figure 4. Hospital CFO Predictions on Capital Spending

- 72 percent of CFOs expect capital spending to increase in the next five years, with the average increase expected to be 14 percent.
- Nearly half of CFOs say they are not keeping up with the capital needs of their deteriorating plants.
- 85 percent of hospital CFOs believe it will be more difficult for their organizations to fund capital expenditures in the future.

Source: Financing the Future Report 6: How Are Hospitals Financing the Future? Where the Industry Will Go from Here. 2004. Healthcare Financial Management Association, Westchester, IL. Reprinted with permission.

FUTURESCAN SURVEY RESULTS: Philanthropy

How likely is it that the following will be seen on a widespread basis (i.e., in the majority of geographic marketplaces) by *2012*?

	Very Likely (%)	Somewhat Likely (%)	Somewhat Unlikely (%)	Very Unlikely (%)
Nonprofit hospitals increasingly will rely on fund-raising to offset operational losses from reduced commercial and government patient care reimbursement	46	38	14	2
Nonprofit hospital CEOs will be evaluated on their involvement in their organizations' fund-raising	27	50	21	2
Nonprofit hospital fund-raisers will increase their focus on major giving programs to significantly increase giving generally	46	48	6	0
Nonprofit hospital fund-raisers will increase their investment in planned giving programs to create a future pipeline of giving	52	43	5	0
Hospitals will increasingly develop long-term (e.g., ten-year) plans for fund-raising, recognizing that major fund-raising campaigns must be developed over time	49	43	7	1
To meet growing donor desire to provide gifts for specific healthcare programs, nonprofit hospital fund-raisers will increase their focus on capital projects and individual programs	52	44	4	0

and undertake technological initiatives that are needed to maintain efficiencies. With the numbers of uninsured and underinsured patients rising and revenues from Medicare and Medicaid decreasing, many hospitals simply do not have the margins to support capital improvements. The future of these hospitals may very much depend on community support and the ability of hospital foundations to harness this support.

A March 2006 Special Comment publication from Moody's Investors Service discusses the growing role foundations play in the financial success of nonprofit hospitals (Martin 2006). This report is an important acknowledgment by the financial community of a significant shift in how fund-raising is viewed in the healthcare field. It is also a tremendous step forward in recognizing the importance of local communities and the influence they have on healthcare delivery through their philanthropy.

Greater Scrutiny for Nonprofit Hospitals

Just as federal Health Insurance Portability and Accountability Act (HIPAA) regulations have had a major effect on hospital and foundation practices, so, too, will the increased scrutiny of nonprofit hospitals' tax-exempt status. The issue is being addressed at both the state and the federal level.

During 2006, for example, the Illinois Attorney General proposed a minimum standard of charity care, based on a measure of 8 percent of the hospital's operating costs, that nonprofit hospitals must meet to maintain tax-exempt status (Madigan 2006)—a wholly unrealistic approach. At the federal level, Senate Finance Committee Chair Charles Grassley (R-IA) has urged the U.S. Treasury Department and the Internal Revenue Service to draft guidance for tax-exempt hospitals regarding charity care requirements (Grassley 2006). The debate over measuring community good will persist into 2007 and most likely beyond. Nonprofit hospitals will continue to come under the scrutiny of the press and politicians who misunderstand the important role hospitals play in the community.

Trends for the Future

To meet the challenge of increased reliance on philanthropy, successful fund-raising programs will become more integrated with the overall business goals of the hospital. This integration will require fundamental changes in the CEO's role in philanthropy as well as in the way hospitals and foundations communicate. Healthcare fund-raisers will focus on ways to be more efficient and obtain greater gains, and to improve how they communicate their organizations' value to the community.

Giving trends will continue to rise. The field is on the right path to meet these new challenges. Healthcare institutions raised an estimated $7.09 billion in total funds in 2005, an increase of 16.3 percent from the previous fiscal year (Association for Healthcare Philanthropy 2006). Not surprisingly, however, it takes more resources to achieve greater results. As a result, productivity in 2005 was at a three-year low, with the median funds raised for each dollar spent dropping to $3.58 (Association for Healthcare Philanthropy 2006). These trends are expected to continue, with more money being spent to achieve greater, but perhaps less efficient, results. Fund-raising staff size will expand, and more money will be invested in technology and in marketing and communication efforts.

Integrating philanthropy into the hospital's strategic plan. In best-practice healthcare organizations, fund-raising has been fully integrated with the overall business strategies of the hospital and, even further, is viewed as a core strategy (Martin 2006). The CEOs are committed to the philanthropic process and actively participate in fund development activities.

The role of the chief development officer (CDO) also is changing. CDOs are being held more accountable for fund-raising performance, and are charged with finding ways to improve results. Engaged development directors are meeting with their hospital counterparts on a regular basis to review activities, analyze results, and discuss strategic and tactical planning.

Healthcare executives have a growing awareness of the need for their increased role in philanthropy. However, although 84 percent of respondents to the *Futurescan* national survey think it is very or somewhat likely that nonprofit hospitals will increasingly rely on fund-raising to offset operational losses, only 77 percent feel strongly that hospital CEOs will be evaluated on their involvement in their organizations' fund-raising programs. Although this gap is not large, it is an indication that many executives have yet to fully grasp the importance of their role.

Changing measures of success. The cost-to-raise-a-dollar benchmark has served healthcare philanthropy for many years and is one indicator of success. However, this negative measure does little to help programs grow to benefit the community served. Although cost to raise a dollar might be a good indication of efficiency, it does not provide the benchmarks necessary to create a more *effective* program. For most foundations, this metric will be just one of many tools used in the future to help guide and evaluate development strategies and plans.

In the coming years, healthcare foundations will begin to adopt the metrics and productivity measures that are prevalent on the clinical side of the hospital. Productivity tools and models, such as the Association for Healthcare Philanthropy's (AHP) benchmarking program, are being created and expanded. We will see more standardization in how fund-raising expenses and revenues are reported, as well as the movement of analytical tools down market to smaller organizations. These tools will become the new standards as organizations continually evaluate and modify resources in response to fund-raising cycles.

Continued shift to major gifts and planned giving. For several years, hospital foundations have been shifting resources to focus more on major gifts to increase giving, and on planned giving to create a future pipeline of funding. This new focus has met with positive results. As shown in Figure 5, funds raised from major gifts increased 17.9 percent in 2005 (from 15.5 percent to 17.8 percent of all giving), while staff time allocated to major gift activities jumped more than 22 percent. Funds raised from planned giving increased from 8.9 percent of all giving in 2004 to 10.4 percent in 2005, a 16.9 percent increase (AHP 2005 and 2006).

Futurescan survey respondents overwhelmingly agree that there will be an increased focus on and investment in major gifts and planned giving programs on a widespread basis in the future, not only to address the increased need for giving, but also to respond to donors' growing desire to provide gifts for specific programs. This shift will require changes in how campaigns are managed and evaluated to accommodate the longer fund-raising cycle.

Focus on community benefit. Whether the solution to the hospital nonprofit status debate is found in industry-dictated

Figure 5. Funds Raised by Type of Fund-Raising Activity

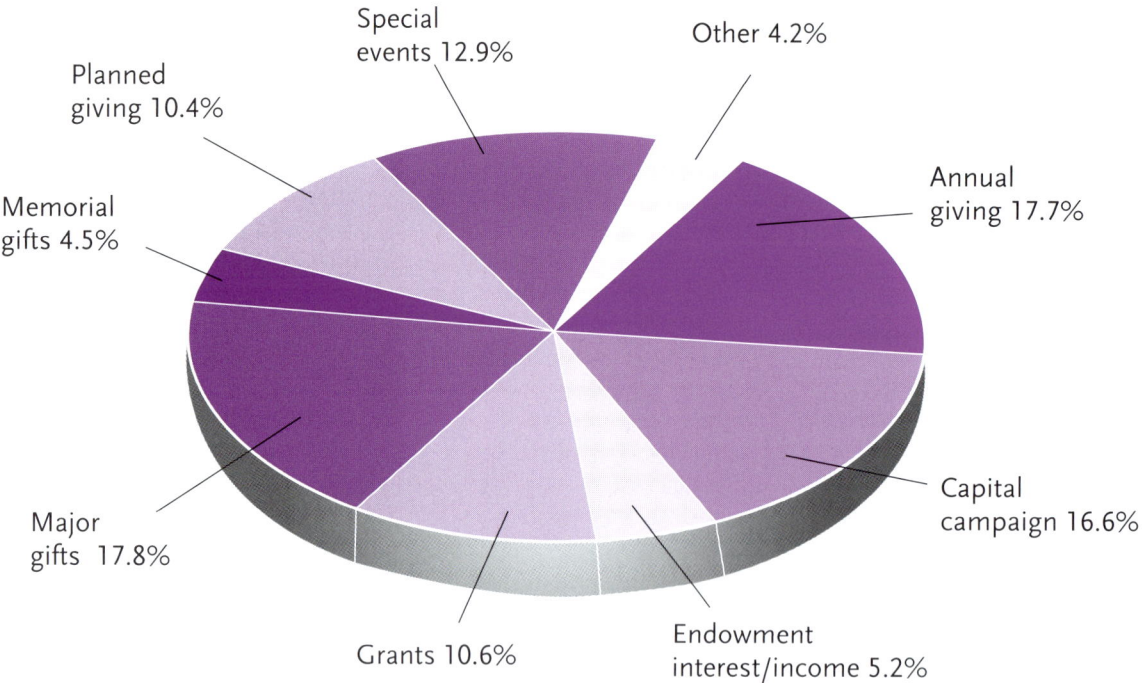

Source: Association for Healthcare Philanthropy. 2006. *FY 2005 Report on Annual Giving USA.* Falls Church, VA: AHP.

standards, such as those outlined by the Catholic Health Association's community benefit guide (CHA 2006), or in federally mandated percentages remains unclear, but the impact on hospitals and foundations is certain.

In the upcoming months, nonprofit hospitals will be engaged in defining and quantifying community good as well as in educating local communities about the benefits that would be lost without nonprofit hospitals. Just as with HIPAA, this effort will most likely require changes in procedures and reporting and investments in additional resources to comply with newly created standards.

This new focus is not necessarily a negative. The increased attention to the question of community benefit will result in much-needed industry standards and improved relationships with local communities as the extensive services provided by nonprofit hospitals are more clearly communicated.

Implications for Hospital Leaders

Hospital leaders must actively address the challenges facing nonprofit hospitals and healthcare philanthropy today to secure a successful future.

Integrate philanthropy as a core strategy. To meet the growing demands on philanthropy, hospital and development executives should work together to integrate philanthropy into the hospital culture. In a best-practice model, the CEO should provide the organizational vision and direction for fund-raising efforts, create an environment for fund development success, and actively participate in fund development activities. The CEO and CDO should be involved in an ex-officio capacity on respective boards. Agreements of association and memorandums of understanding that outline the relationship between the two organizations should be created or reviewed to ensure that this new model is outlined and supported.

Adopt better measurements and standards. With the growing emphasis on major gift campaigns and the shift to longer-term philanthropy cycles, hospital and development executives must develop long-term plans as well as meaningful standards and tools to facilitate better decision making and more effective resource allocation. The CDO, working closely with the hospital CEO and CFO, should

20   FUTURESCAN

evaluate healthcare philanthropy best practices and benchmarks and invest in adopting and integrating these tools. Healthcare fund-raisers who embrace a more scientific approach to the art of philanthropy will be in a position to respond as capital needs increase. Those who do not will have difficulty meeting the ever-rising challenges.

Use technology to improve efficiency. Fund-raising organizations will increasingly be asked to generate more with less, so improving efficiency and effectiveness will be critical for success. CDOs should evaluate the long-term benefits of adopting technologies such as enhanced donor management software systems, wealth matching and modeling for prospect identification, and online fund-raising. The continued shift to major gift programs will require better donor identification and segmentation so that targeted messages can be created to improve results.

Develop a plan to communicate community benefit. Nonprofit hospital executives and development officers should begin now to review industry resources, such as the Catholic Health Association's *A Guide for Planning and Reporting Community Benefit* (CHA 2006), and develop a plan to identify and quantify community benefit. Assume that there will be more government involvement sooner rather than later, and get ahead of the curve. Create an integrated public relations and marketing strategy to educate the community, and have a plan in place to address negative reports from the local press or politicians. The increased positive awareness you create will only strengthen your case for support and enhance your fund-raising efforts.

References

Association for Healthcare Philanthropy. 2006. *FY 2005 Report on Giving USA*. Falls Church, VA: AHP.

———. 2005. *FY 2004 Report on Giving USA*. Falls Church, VA: AHP.

Catholic Health Association of the United States. 2006. *A Guide for Planning and Reporting Community Benefit*. St. Louis, MO: CHA.

Grassley, C. 2006. "Grassley Directs Effort to Ensure More Charitable Care from Non-profit Hospitals." [Online press release; created 9/13/06; retrieved 10/20/06.] http://grassley.senate.gov

Madigan, L. 2006. "Madigan Proposes Two Bills to Hold Hospitals Accountable for Charity Care, Stop Unfair Billing and Collection Practices." [Online press release; created 1/23/06; retrieved 10/20/06.]http://www.illinoisattorney general.gov/pressroom/2006_01/20060123.html

Martin, A. 2006. *Fundraising at Not-for-Profit Hospitals Largely Untapped but Increasing: Strong Philanthropy Strengthens Bond Ratings*. Special Comment. New York: Moody's Investors Service.

5. PHYSICIANS: A STABILIZING OF THE SOCIAL CONTRACT WITH HOSPITALS

by Thomas C. Royer, M.D.

About the Author
Thomas C. Royer, M.D., is chief executive officer and president of CHRISTUS Health, based in Dallas, Texas. Dr. Royer has extensive expertise in developing physician partnerships and community health programs within CHRISTUS. In his nearly seven years with the organization, he has led CHRISTUS Health through a remarkable period of growth, making it one of the ten largest Catholic health systems in the nation today. In 2006, he was named the Seventh Most Powerful Physician Executive in Healthcare by *Modern Physician* magazine. Before joining CHRISTUS Health in 1999, Dr. Royer served as senior vice president of medical affairs of the Henry Ford Health System and chairman of the board of governors of Henry Ford Medical Group, both in Detroit. A board-certified surgeon, Dr. Royer received his medical degree from the University of Pennsylvania in Philadelphia and completed his postdoctoral training at Geisinger Medical Center and Clinic in Danville, Pennsylvania.

Although the daily crises in healthcare can be difficult to solve and can absorb much time and energy, healthcare leaders today must take the longer view and attempt to envision the future for the next decade. This longer time frame is essential for three reasons:

1. Technology is being developed and implemented rapidly in all segments of healthcare.
2. Research in prevalent diseases is transferring knowledge more rapidly to the bedside, eradicating or curing some diseases and minimizing the severity of others.
3. The profile of the aging population is showing a much healthier group of people, not aging like their parents but living more active and productive lives and living a greater number of senior years.

These three major drivers of healthcare change are causing, not unexpectedly, a significant amount of anxiety for physicians, because they are affecting where and how physicians will be delivering their services. In addition, these necessary changes will continue to further stress what are often already strained relationships between physicians and hospitals.

For the past ten years, reimbursement methodologies, particularly those of governmental payers, have pitted hospitals and doctors against one another, often shifting income from one group to the other because of the overall decline in the federal and state health spending budgets. As a result, unhealthy competition from physicians has been increasing. This is seen in physician ownership of outpatient surgical centers, radiology services, other specialty programs, and niche hospitals.

In addition, data made public recently show a lack of uniformity of care provided by both physicians and hospitals—care that is often below acceptable standards. This has led to finger pointing, negativity, and passive-aggressive behaviors.

Consequently, physicians and hospital leadership have had difficulty both recognizing the need for and achieving a balance between effectiveness, efficiency, and fiscal stability in the delivery of healthcare services. That has resulted in the unhealthy competition referred to above, causing decreased financial gains for all concerned.

Changing Physician Demographics
Clearly, the answer going forward must be for hospitals and physicians to reach consensus on the challenges they face and seek compromise solutions. This is challenging, because there is no common voice among physicians

FUTURESCAN SURVEY RESULTS: PHYSICIANS

How likely is it that the following will be seen on a widespread basis (i.e., in the majority of geographic marketplaces) by *2012*?

	Very Likely (%)	Somewhat Likely (%)	Somewhat Unlikely (%)	Very Unlikely (%)
Physician-hospital relationships will improve over the next five years	8	40	45	7
Gain-sharing plans* will be a major factor in improving physician-hospital relationships in the next five years	10	48	37	5
Hospitals will find it easier to develop good relations with younger physicians than older physicians	25	47	25	3
The legal arrangements between hospitals and doctors will increase in both number and complexity	54	42	4	0
The increasing number of physicians in group practices will make it easier for hospitals to develop win-win relationship models	10	46	39	5

* Gain sharing is a method that compensates individuals based on improvements in an organization's productivity. Because such compensation is only implemented when gains are achieved, gain-sharing plans do not adversely affect an organization's costs.

today, and none will be heard in the future.

What we see will be enhanced differences of opinion between older and younger physicians, specialists and primary care physicians, surgeons and internists and hospitalists, employed doctors and private practitioners, and men and women physicians. Turf battles between specialties will increase. There will be more gender and ethnic diversity, fewer independent practitioners, and shortages in key specialties. Differences of opinion among physicians will only accelerate as physicians seek alternative income sources and new business models and as gender and ethnic diversity increases.

A Stabilizing Relationship with Hospitals

In the next decade, because of changes in and even reversal of regulations concerning physician equity models in healthcare, the unraveling that has recently occurred in the social contract between physicians and hospitals will begin to stabilize. Physicians will choose to invest with hospitals in joint-venture projects in which each will have opportunities to participate and to make management decisions. Win-win outcomes are hoped for, for each group will have an ownership interest.

Forty-eight percent of *Futurescan* survey respondents believe it is very or somewhat likely that physician-hospital relationships will improve over the next five years. Nearly three-quarters of respondents say that hospitals will find it easier to develop good relations with younger physicians than with older ones. In addition:

- Many physicians will stop working in hospitals entirely. The critical patients remaining in the hospitals of the future will be cared for mainly by hospitalists, intensivists, neonatologists, and perinatologists.
- Physicians who today are seeking alternative income sources and pursuing new business models (frequently in competition with hospitals) will slowly seek partnerships with hospitals again. Fifty-eight percent of *Futurescan* survey respondents believe that gain-sharing plans will be a major factor in improving physician-hospital relationships in the next five years.
- More physicians will seek employed models once again. An overwhelming 96 percent of *Futurescan* survey respondents believe it is likely that the legal arrangements between hospitals and doctors will increase in both number and complexity.

New Models of Care Delivery

Even with all the advancements in healthcare that will become a reality in the next decade, the number of uninsured will continue to increase, particularly among younger people, who often do not see healthcare insurance as a high budget priority. In addition, many more companies will reduce healthcare coverage for their retirees, a large number of whom will choose, or be forced, to have little or no insurance.

Consequently, new healthcare delivery models will of necessity be developed to provide basic healthcare for the underserved and uninsured, with a strong emphasis on chronic care management and wellness service lines. These clinics will be necessary to decrease the large numbers of patients now being seen in emergency rooms, an expensive and unsatisfactory care setting for the "walking wounded." Significant changes will be required in the traditional roles of hospital emergency departments, emergency physicians, and specialists covering emergency calls.

Concentrating on disease management and preventive care will be foreign to some physicians and hospitals. Until reimbursement for such services becomes adequate, physicians and hospitals will not rapidly embrace these new ways.

Transparency

Demands for transparency will increase from all the voices calling for change in healthcare—government, business, payers, patients, and families. As the cost of healthcare continues to rise and an increasing portion of the payment becomes the personal obligation of the patient, these voices will demand to see that they are getting value that, in some fashion, parallels the cost of the service. Pay for performance is being rapidly embraced and is seen as a necessary alignment of incentives to achieve excellence in quality and service delivery. Both physicians and hospitals will be required to share their individual and collective outcomes as the future unfolds.

Implications for Hospital Leaders

In summary, physician-hospital relationships, a critical factor for access to high-quality and affordable care, will continue to change, it is hoped for the better. The implications for hospital leaders include the following.

Physicians must be heard. Hospital leaders should work with key medical staff leaders to ensure that physicians have a representative voice to assist in formulating the physicians' perspectives on healthcare change. Hospital leaders should engage physicians in dialogue about how the two groups can mutually help one another and work collaboratively. Periodic physician surveys are helpful in assessing the physicians' perspectives and in formulating action plans to enhance relationships.

Physician-hospital alignment. Hospitals should develop and nurture relationships with their medical staffs and evaluate hospital policies, plans, and procedures to ensure that physicians are aware of them. In addition, seeking physicians' input as to the extent to which they would like to be involved is important.

Both hospitals and physicians should seek to ensure that the solutions create a win-win scenario for both parties. More than half of *Futurescan* survey respondents said it was very or somewhat likely that the increasing number of physicians in group practices will make it easier to develop win-win relationship models.

The quality imperative. Once hospitals have identified key quality measures and focused their systems and processes on those measures that will drive the institution's reimbursement levels under pay for performance, they should train physician leaders in quality, improvements in existing systems and processes, and how to effectively manage change. Both hospitals and physicians must do whatever is necessary to create excellence for all patients whom they encounter together. This should be a shared goal.

These most important implications must have well-defined strategies to ensure the best possible future for our patients, community residents, and their families.

6. QUALITY AND SAFETY: COMPETITION BECOMES A MARKET REALITY

by Janet M. Corrigan, Ph.D., and Cara S. Lesser

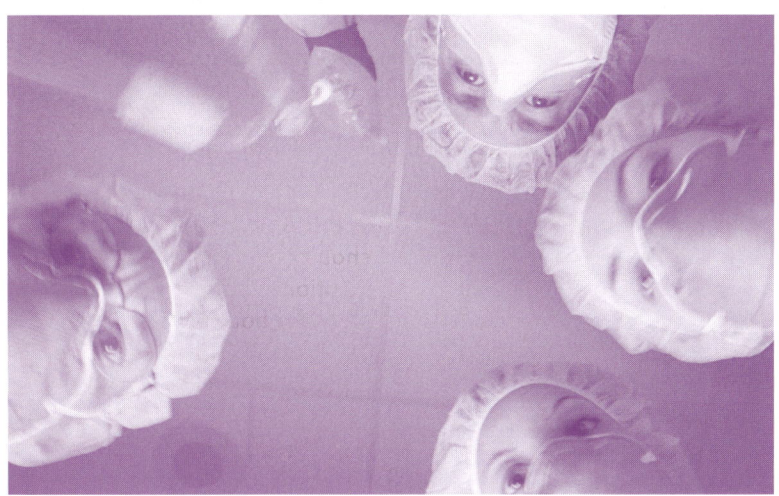

About the Authors

Janet M. Corrigan, Ph.D., is president and CEO of the National Quality Forum (NQF), a private, not-for-profit membership organization established in 1999 to develop and implement a national strategy for healthcare quality measurement and reporting. Dr. Corrigan was instrumental in organizing the merger between NQF and the National Committee for Quality Health Care (NCQHC), where she served as president and CEO from June 2005 to March 2006. Before that, she was senior board director at the Institute of Medicine (IOM), with responsibility for its Health Care Services portfolio of initiatives. Dr. Corrigan received the IOM's Cecil Award for Distinguished Service in 2002 and is a fellow in the American College of Medical Informatics. She received her doctorate in health services research from the University of Michigan in Ann Arbor.

Cara Lesser is vice president of the NQF Executive Institute, a new education and outreach initiative to engage executives and board members of healthcare organizations to dramatically improve quality of care. Ms. Lesser came to NQF from the Center for Studying Health System Change, where she directed the organization's "site visit"–based research. In 2006 she received the first AcademyHealth Health Services Research Impact Award for outstanding examples of the positive impact of research on health policy or practice. Ms. Lesser received her master's degree in public policy from the University of California at Berkeley.

In the first half of this decade, quality and safety were put on the map as critical problems for the U.S. healthcare system to confront, with healthcare leaders, policymakers, and payers laying the foundation for change. In the next five years, we will see tremendous progress in making quality improvement and patient safety a reality, as well as a growing market and regulatory imperative for healthcare systems to demonstrate their performance in these areas.

Are We Making Progress?

Some recent reports on the state of the healthcare system are discouraging about how little ground we have gained over the past five years, despite increased attention to these problems. The Commonwealth Fund's national scorecard on the performance of the U.S. healthcare system reinforced that we can no longer operate under the assumption that we have the best healthcare system in the world. Among 19 industrialized countries, the United States ranked 15th on "mortality from conditions amenable to healthcare"—deaths before age 75 that are potentially preventable with timely, effective care. The U.S. rate was more than 30 percent worse than the benchmark set by the top three countries. The United States also ranks at the bottom for healthy life expectancy, and last on infant mortality (Schoen et al. 2006).

At the same time, the estimated number of deaths due to medical errors appears to be even higher than originally reported in the Institute of Medicine's galvanizing report *To Err Is Human* (IOM 2006; Leape and Berwick 2005; IOM 2000). The typical adult still has only slightly better than a 50-50 chance of receiving recommended medical care (McGlynn et al. 2003). Minorities receive lower-quality care for both routine medical care and specialty care, even after accounting for differences in insurance status and income level (IOM 2002).

However, focusing only on the tremendous gaps that remain in quality of care and patient safety risks overlooking the very important accomplishments over the past few years that lay the groundwork for transformational change. Payers, policymakers, and healthcare

FUTURESCAN SURVEY RESULTS: QUALITY AND SAFETY

How likely is it that the following will be seen on a widespread basis (i.e., in the majority of geographic marketplaces) by **2012**?

	Very Likely (%)	Somewhat Likely (%)	Somewhat Unlikely (%)	Very Unlikely (%)
Patients will become savvy shoppers for healthcare, balancing cost and quality considerations	27	47	23	3
Most chronic care patients will have personal health records that enable them to track health behaviors and symptoms, communicate with clinicians via e-mail, and access clinical guidelines and evidence	19	50	28	3
Multispecialty group practice will become the practice setting of choice for physicians as evidence grows substantiating its superior quality	22	51	25	2
Multispecialty group practice will become the care setting of choice for patients as evidence grows substantiating its superior quality	19	51	27	3
Hospitals with higher-than-expected mortality rates for routine surgical procedures will lose market share because of publicly disclosed quality metrics	33	50	16	1

leaders have stepped up to the plate and are putting in place the building blocks necessary to mobilize and sustain change. In just the past couple of years, we have seen Medicare entice almost every hospital in the nation to publicly report data on clinical quality by tying a 0.4 percent payment update to participation. Pay for performance has become an accepted and widely adopted strategy to align incentives to reduce costs and improve quality of care (Trude, Au, and Christianson 2006).

National organizations have made great strides in establishing the infrastructure to support these initiatives with standardized quality measures, and in the development and rapid diffusion of evidence-based best practices to optimize quality and patient safety. The success of the Institute for Healthcare Improvement's recent 100,000 Lives Campaign is testament to the fact that healthcare leaders are ready, willing, and able to rise to the challenge to dramatically improve the quality of healthcare—and they are ready to do it now (Hackbarth, McCannon, and Berwick 2006).

Raising the Bar and Raising the Stakes

What's to come in the next five years? In a word: more. We will see more public reporting, more financial incentives, and more professional pressure to improve quality. Specifically, we will see:

- More states and local entities getting into public reporting
- An expanded set of standardized measures for public reporting and performance assessment that cover a broader range of clinical conditions, care settings, and aspects of quality, such as efficiency and equity
- More longitudinal measures that shift the focus from discrete encounters with the healthcare system to episodes of care that encompass a range of inpatient, outpatient, home-based, and preventive services
- More composite measures that integrate multiple indicators of provider performance
- More consumer-friendly approaches to communicating provider performance data, and greater emphasis on making the information useful for patients when they are in a position to make decisions about where to seek care
- More use of pay for performance—for both hospitals

and physicians—and a greater portion of payment at risk
- More health plan "steering" to high-performing providers via increasingly differentiated copays and coinsurance that start to get patients' attention
- More stringent accreditation and professional certification requirements and review processes to ensure quality at both the institutional and the individual practitioner level
- More public campaigns to drive progress in the healthcare system as a whole, and more public scrutiny and pressure to demonstrate results

Implications for Hospital Leaders

Together these changes will push quality and patient safety over the tipping point, making it more important than ever for hospital and health system leaders to be on top of their game with respect to managing, ensuring, and documenting quality of care. For those who have not already embraced quality as a strategic imperative, it will become critical to do so. Those who are already ahead of the curve will face greater competitive pressure to stay out in front.

We see three key strategies for hospital and health system leaders to respond to this environment.

Strengthen partnerships with physicians. The widening scope of performance measures that will be publicly reported and used to determine reimbursement and direct patient volume will make it more important than ever to tighten relationships with physicians to enhance care coordination and improve system performance. Physicians themselves are going to face mounting pressure from reduced Medicare fees, pay for performance, health plan network designs, and public reporting. Increasingly, they will be at a crossroads as to how to maintain income and manage information demands under current practice arrangements.

In this context, physicians will become more open to exploring new organizational arrangements that can position them to succeed in a quality- and performance-driven environment. A substantial majority of *Futurescan* survey respondents believe that multispecialty group practice will become the practice setting of choice for both physicians and patients as evidence grows of its superior quality. Other arrangements are likely to emerge as well to provide increasingly important organizational supports such as electronic health records, patient and clinician prompts and reminders, multidisciplinary teams, and health promotion and disease prevention programs. In the next few years, we will see a great deal of experimenting with different approaches to establish this infrastructure—whether through multispecialty groups, closer alignment of physicians with hospitals, or development of more loosely structured virtual systems—with different paths likely to emerge depending on the particular characteristics of the community.

Understand and manage the link between quality and financial performance in your organization. Hospital and health system leaders will be pressed to become much more sophisticated about managing the link between financial performance and quality in the next few years, and now is the time to develop and refine systems to do this. Three out of four *Futurescan* survey respondents believe that patients will become savvy shoppers for healthcare, balancing cost and quality considerations, and more than four out of five survey respondents say that hospitals with higher-than-expected mortality rates for routine surgical procedures will lose market share because of publicly disclosed quality metrics. Although it remains to be seen how price information will be conveyed to patients and if this occurs on a widespread basis, the combination of public reporting, pay for performance, and health plan benefit design has the strength to move market share, particularly if and when these strategies become increasingly aligned.

Hospital and health system leaders will need sophisticated dashboards that integrate an assessment of performance on key measures of clinical quality and patient safety with financial performance indicators to stay on top of their game. In addition, hospital and health system leaders will need to adopt new approaches to management and board oversight to strengthen their ability to effectively steer their organizations in this environment.

Offer an electronic patient health record. Many hospitals and health systems are in the process of evaluating or rolling out some form of electronic health record to manage patient information across settings. Some organizations, however, are getting out ahead of the game by offering a patient health record (PHR) "overlay" that not only assists patients and their families in carrying out treatment plans and keeping up with preventive health services, but also provides many features to help manage patient care across the continuum of services and optimize clinician time—features that will become increasingly important in the evolving healthcare market. For instance, a PHR offers a mechanism to provide preventive care reminders, easily share information about clinical guidelines and evidence, track health behaviors and symptoms, and support e-mail communication with clinicians.

Almost 70 percent of *Futurescan* survey respondents believe that most chronic care patients will have a PHR by 2012—a figure that underscores strong professional support for the potential value of this tool. Hospitals and health systems should work collaboratively with other providers and health plans in their community to make PHRs available to all patients. Although the underlying data about a patient's care should belong to the patient and be portable, the power of PHRs rests in their ability to integrate the "record" of a patient's health experience with the clinicians and institutions that provide care to make it an interactive tool to support and streamline the care delivery process. Hospital and health system leadership will be needed to make this a reality.

References

Hackbarth, A.D., C.J. McCannon, and D.M. Berwick. 2006. "Interpreting the 'Lives Saved' Result of IHI's 100,000 Lives Campaign." *Joint Commission Benchmark* 8 (5): 1–11.

Institute of Medicine. 2000. *To Err is Human: Building a Safer Health System*. Washington, DC: National Academies Press.

———. 2002. *Unequal Treatment: Confronting Racial and Ethnic Disparities in Health Care*. Washington, DC: National Academies Press.

———. 2006. *Preventing Medical Errors: Quality Chasm Series*. Washington, DC: National Academies Press.

Leape, L.L., and D.M. Berwick. 2005. "Five Years After *To Err is Human*: What Have We Learned?" *Journal of the American Medical Association* 293 (19): 2384–90.

McGlynn, E.A., S.M. Asch, J. Adams, J. Keesey, J. Hicks, A. DeCristofaro, and E.A. Kerr. 2003. "The Quality of Health Care Delivered to Adults in the United States." *New England Journal of Medicine* 348 (26): 2635–45.

Schoen, C., K. Davis, S.K.H. How, and S.C. Schoenbaum. 2006. "U.S. Health System Performance: A National Scorecard." *Health Affairs* Web Exclusive [Online article; created 9/20/06; retrieved 9/20/06.] http://content.healthaffairs.org/cgi/content/abstract/hlthaff.25.w457.

Trude, S., M. Au, and J.B. Christianson. 2006. "Health Plan Pay-for-Performance Strategies." *American Journal of Managed Care* 12 (9): 537–42.

7. CLINICAL TECHNOLOGY: CONFRONTING THE TECHNOLOGICAL IMPERATIVE

by Lawton R. Burns, Ph.D.

About the Author

Lawton R. Burns, Ph.D., is the James Joo-Jin Kim Professor and professor of health care systems in the Wharton School at the University of Pennsylvania in Philadelphia. Dr. Burns is also director of the Wharton Center for Health Management and Economics. He has served on the governing board of the Institute of Medicine (Health Services section) and the editorial board of *Health Services Research*, and he is a past member of the Grant Review Study Section of the Agency for Health Care Policy and Research. He is also a life fellow of Clare Hall at the University of Cambridge in England. Dr. Burns's recent publications include a book on supply chain management in the healthcare field, *The Health Care Value Chain* (Jossey-Bass, 2002), and a companion volume on *The Business of Healthcare Innovation* (Cambridge University Press, 2005). He received his doctorate in sociology and his M.B.A. in health administration from the University of Chicago.

New technology—its introduction and its use—has accounted for 20 to 40 percent of the annual rise in U.S. healthcare spending since 1960, as shown in Figure 6 (Burns 2005). Clinical technology is commonly cited as the major driver of rising expenditures worldwide. Observers and researchers have characterized this trend as the *technological imperative:* the demand by patients and their physicians for access to the latest equipment and procedures on the grounds of quality, coupled with the willingness of third parties to pay for them. Recent research suggests that this increased spending over the last part of the twentieth century has provided reasonable value measured in terms of increased life

Figure 6. Technology as Share of Annual Percentage Increases in U.S. Personal Health Expenditures, 1961–1998

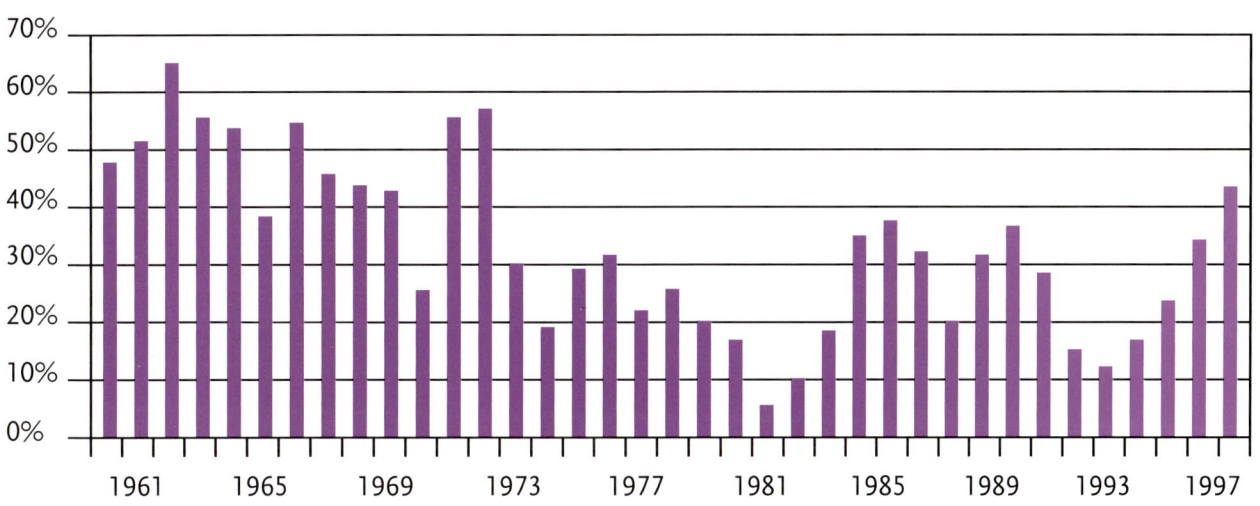

Source: Data from Center for Medicare & Medicaid Services (CMS). Reprinted in Burns, *The Business of Healthcare Innovation*, 2005.

FUTURESCAN SURVEY RESULTS: CLINICAL TECHNOLOGY

How likely is it that the following will be seen on a widespread basis (i.e., in the majority of geographic marketplaces) by **2012**?

	Very Likely (%)	Somewhat Likely (%)	Somewhat Unlikely (%)	Very Unlikely (%)
The flow of new technology into the hospital will continue unabated	55	36	8	1
Medicare reimbursement for high-cost technologies and procedures will increase to catch up with rising hospital expenditures on technology	2	17	58	23
Vendors of new technological products will help hospitals use their limited capital budgets more efficiently (e.g., by providing information to help hospitals forecast and budget for new products)	11	50	34	5
Specialist physicians will partner with the hospitals in which they practice to control the cost and utilization of new, expensive technology	12	50	34	5
Hospitals will develop new-technology committees to evaluate new products	40	50	10	0
New-technology committees will be able to assess the patient safety risks of new technology	19	58	22	1

expectancy (Cutler, Rosen, and Vijan 2006).

What has not been carefully considered, however, is the impact of the technological imperative on hospitals. The American Hospital Association's Annual Survey tracks the adoption and prevalence of specific clinical technologies, but gives no insight into their impact or implications. In the past, new clinical technologies might have been associated with higher revenues and margins. However, because of the rising costs of new products and the failure of Medicare reimbursement to keep up with those costs, the presence of clinical technologies can result in breakeven operations or even losses. This suggests that hospital executives must carefully and deliberately manage the technological imperative. There is now a *managerial imperative* to deal with the technological imperative.

This section of *Futurescan* describes how hospital executives view the future flow of clinical technology and assesses the strategies needed to manage it. The results suggest that the managerial imperative will become critical by 2012.

Charting the Technological Imperative

Based on figures from Solucient and consultants, the cost of technological and other supplies to U.S. hospitals grew at an 8 percent compound average growth rate (CAGR) during the 1990s (Solucient 2005). Analysts labeled this "uncontrolled growth." Part of the rise reflects the continuing flow of new drug applications and significant medical device breakthroughs monitored by the Food and Drug Administration's various centers. Many of these devices came with astonishingly high price tags (e.g., $25,000 for an implanted cardioverter defibrillator, or ICD). When one combines the high price of ICDs with the increased demand that results from expanded patient indications for Medicare ICD coverage, the explanation for rising costs due to clinical technology becomes more straightforward. Indeed, Figure 7 illustrates that the rise in healthcare spending as a percentage of U.S. gross domestic product (GDP) tracks the introduction of new medical devices.

Defining the Managerial Imperative

The problem for hospitals is that oftentimes the cost of the product consumes the bulk of Medicare reimbursement, leaving

Figure 7. Introduction of Medical Devices and Rise of Healthcare Spending, 1900-2000

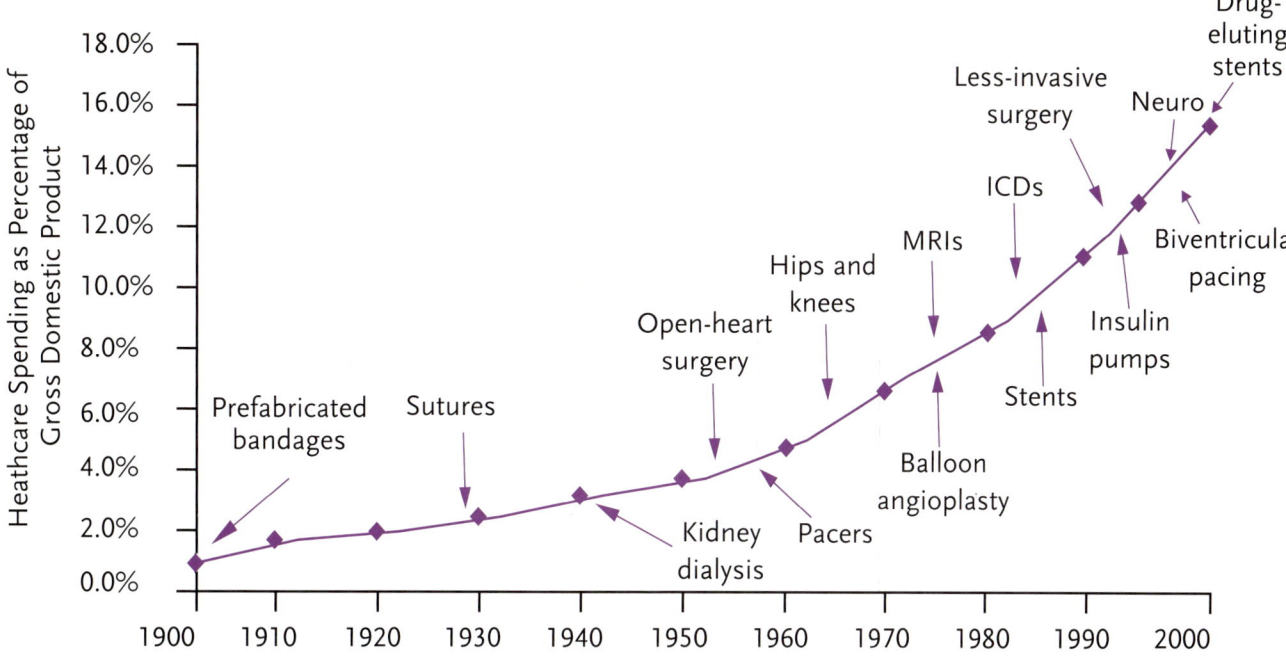

Source: Kurt Kruger. Presentation to Wharton School, November 2005.

little left over to cover other operating expenses, let alone contribute to margins. A comparison of orthopedic implant prices and reimbursement levels, and their disparate growth rates over the past few years, illustrates the point.

The implications of ICDs, orthopedic implants, and other clinical technologies for hospital executives are clear: executives must (1) lobby for more adequate Medicare reimbursement, or at least greater visibility of device pricing, (2) work more closely with physician specialists to manage the procurement and utilization of these technologies, and (3) collaborate with suppliers to manage the costs of the technologies themselves and the high costs of technology service lines. This threefold task constitutes the managerial imperative.

Hospital Executives' Views
Respondents to this year's *Futurescan* survey recognize the issues outlined above. More than 90 percent of respondents believe it is somewhat likely or very likely that the flow of new clinical technology into their hospitals will continue unabated over the next several years, continuing the pattern observed over the past 40 to 50 years. A similar percentage feels that hospitals will develop new-technology committees to screen and evaluate these new products as they are introduced. A somewhat smaller percentage (77 percent), however, believes that these committees will be able to assess the patient safety risks of this new technology; indeed, only 19 percent feel this is very likely to happen. That is, hospitals will be bombarded with a continuing cascade of new products for which the patient safety risks are unlikely to be known. Hospitals are also likely to lack good information on the overall quality profile of these products.

Where can hospitals turn for help? Only 12 percent of respondents think it very likely that hospitals will partner with their physician specialists to control the cost and utilization of these high-technology products, and only 11 percent think it very likely that the vendors of these products will help hospitals use their limited budgets to order and utilize new technology more efficiently. Only 2 percent think it very likely that Medicare reimbursement for these products will keep pace with their rising costs.

Implications for Hospital Leaders
Hospital executives are not very optimistic about their ability to handle the managerial imperative. One reason may be the traditional lack of attention paid to supply chain and technology issues. This inattention has some obvious roots: preoccupation with managed care payers (rather than vendors), especially during the 1990s; lack of background and training in supply chain management; lack of

understanding of the technology sectors; and possibly a failure to fully grasp the business model and practices of technology vendors. Another reason is the close partnership between physicians and vendors, coupled with the hospital's historical problems in working with both of them.

Support for better reimbursement and price transparency. Hospital executives will need to attend to these issues more closely if they wish to confront the technological imperative. External efforts to lobby the government for higher reimbursement on high-technology-intensive procedures may or may not succeed. Recent experience with changes in Medicare reimbursement for such procedures suggests that providers can delay but not escape reductions in payment.

Parallel with any such lobbying efforts, hospitals should pressure the Centers for Medicare and Medicaid Services (CMS) to publicize prices of devices and other technologies that the government pays for—and link this campaign to the burgeoning effort elsewhere to make provider prices more visible and transparent. In so doing, hospitals may also do a better job of educating Congress that their Medicare reimbursement levels can be largely consumed by the prices they have to pay for new technology.

Hospitals may also wish to support current private-sector efforts by technology assessment firms such as ECRI and Aspen Healthcare Metrics to make device pricing more transparent and visible. By doing so, providers can then share this information with physicians in their cost-containment efforts or bargain more effectively with vendors.

Policing the introduction of new products. On the internal front, hospitals will need to devote more staff resources to scrutinizing all of the new clinical technology that seeks to enter the hospital and the practices of physicians working in the hospital. The following lessons from the University of Pennsylvania Health System are instructive. The mere presence of a new-technology committee is not enough; the committee *process* is what is important. The new-technology committee should include primarily physicians (not just nurses and other clinicians) from the different hospital areas where new technologies are used. These physicians then police the introduction of new products by their colleagues. A physician who wants a new technology must persuade his or her colleagues, not hospital administration.

Such committees should require any physician who wants to introduce a new technology to submit a spreadsheet that lays out the cost and revenue generation implications for the hospital, as well as all published studies on the product's efficacy compared with current technology. Confronting the cost of such technologies can oftentimes be an "aha!" moment for physicians. The committee process thus instills in its members a cost and quality discipline and fosters greater surveillance over new product introductions.

These committees are not designed to prevent access to new technologies desired by physicians and their patients. Indeed, experience shows that a majority of new technologies brought before such committees are approved. However, the handful of times that committees reject new technologies sought by physicians sends a signal to the medical staff that the hospital is serious about the process and that new product introductions must be defended. Rejections also send a message to vendors that the hospital can be tough on vendors with flimsy claims about breakthrough technologies. Finally, the process serves to pare down and slow down the otherwise irresistible flow of new technology into the facility.

Monitoring vendors. The internal effort should also include stepped-up efforts to monitor what sales representatives bring inside the institution, particularly in high-cost areas such as the operating room and the cath lab. Greater supervision of these areas may be rewarded by the savings reaped from limiting vendor placement of new items on shelves before they have been placed on contract.

New-product trials. The internal effort should also include the trial of new products before they are purchased. Vendors wishing to introduce new products should submit to in-house clinical trials conducted by the hospital, not the vendor, and should donate their products for these trials. In this manner, the hospital can gather more rigorous clinical and economic evidence on new products, rather than relying on vendor marketing claims and vendor-sponsored and vendor-conducted studies. Moreover, these trials should include head-to-head comparisons of leading brands (and any breakthrough technologies, if they exist). Such comparisons are woefully lacking in the arena of technology assessment.

Recognition of materials management and purchasing. Finally, the managerial imperative includes a recognition that functions heretofore relegated to the basement and the loading dock—materials management and purchasing—are key operating areas of the hospital that account for up to 30 percent of the hospital's expenses and represent the last frontier for cost containment and margin improvement. The materials and purchasing managers of today may be in the same position as the personnel managers of the 1970s and 1980s—overlooked managers destined to rise from the basement and assume vital roles in the hospital.

References

Burns, L.R. 2005. *The Business of Healthcare Innovation*. Cambridge, UK: Cambridge University Press.

Cutler, D.M., A.B. Rosen, and S. Vijan. 2006. "The Value of Medical Spending in the United States, 1960–2000." *New England Journal of Medicine* 355 (9): 920–27.

Solucient. 2005. *The Comparative Performance of U.S. Hospitals: The 2005 Sourcebook*. Evanston, IL: Solucient.

8. INFORMATION TECHNOLOGY: MOVING TOWARD AN ELECTRONIC MEDICAL RECORD

by Thomas M. Priselac and Darren Dworkin

About the Authors

Thomas M. Priselac is president and chief executive officer of the Cedars-Sinai Health System in Los Angeles, a position he has held since 1994. Mr. Priselac is chair of the Association of American Medical Colleges (AAMC), a former member of the board of trustees of the American Hospital Association, and a past chair of the Hospital Association of Southern California, the California Healthcare Association, and the AAMC's Council of Teaching Hospitals. He is also a member of the boards of Charles R. Drew University in Los Angeles and the Los Angeles Chamber of Commerce, where he chairs the Health Care Committee. The holder of the Warschaw/Law Endowed Chair in Healthcare Leadership at Cedars-Sinai Medical Center, Mr. Priselac is also an adjunct assistant professor at the U.C.L.A. School of Public Health. He holds a master's degree in public health, health services administration, and planning from the University of Pittsburgh.

Darren Dworkin is vice president of enterprise information systems and chief information officer of the Cedars-Sinai Health System in Los Angeles, California. Mr. Dworkin has spent 15 years in information technology and 6 in healthcare. Before joining Cedars-Sinai, he held the position of chief technology officer at the Boston University Medical Center, where he led the development and deployment of an infrastructure and application framework to bring technology to the point of care. Mr. Dworkin has been a leader in helping major information technology vendors bring solutions to the healthcare marketplace, enabling improvements in workflow and quality in provider settings.

The economics of healthcare are increasingly demanding. Healthcare providers are challenged to continually improve the productivity of their practices even as they must spend more time documenting and reporting on the care they deliver. They must effectively meet the often-conflicting demands of payers, regulators, and patients. These pressures affect not only the way providers use their time, but also their financial health and their ability to deliver quality care.

Given this complex environment, the promise of the electronic medical record (EMR) is being touted more and more as part of the solution. The benefits of the EMR are often cited, the assumption being that dynamic or even dramatic results will follow EMR adoption. The initial expectations are simple, along the lines of cost savings from fewer chart pulls and major reductions in transcription costs. Less visible at first, but equally significant, are the elimination of potential duplicate tests and the opportunities for more accurate coding, improved clinical productivity, and more complete clinical documentation. Finally, with rich repositories of data derived from implemented EMRs comes the possibility of information sharing and the ability to enhance the clinical practice of medicine, with the attendant quality and cost benefits.

The question remains, why is it taking so long? It is hard to imagine that the slow adoption of the EMR is from a lack of will or desire. It is increasingly difficult to find a healthcare publication that does not trumpet the benefits of information technology (IT). The popular press, major corporations, and most levels of government all have outlined the need for an accelerated healthcare IT agenda. With this strong demand, what will be the necessary steps to move us forward?

Advancements in Technology

Not that long ago, computer systems in healthcare meant proprietary hardware and software tied to a device or modality with a specialized function. If an application in the healthcare setting was identified, a vendor would go to work to build every aspect of the

FUTURESCAN SURVEY RESULTS: INFORMATION TECHNOLOGY

How likely is it that the following will be seen on a widespread basis (i.e., in the majority of geographic marketplaces) by **2012**?

	Very Likely (%)	Somewhat Likely (%)	Somewhat Unlikely (%)	Very Unlikely (%)
Removal of governmental financial barriers that limit how hospitals can provide technology to physicians will encourage electronic medical record (EMR) adoption	21	50	25	4
Quality and outcome measures, including new payer reporting requirements, will be key drivers of EMR adoption	34	52	13	1
Federal/state interoperability and standards initiatives will remove barriers and encourage EMR adoption	15	52	30	3
Continued advancements in technology (e.g., PCs, wireless, voice recognition) will be key drivers of EMR adoption	44	48	8	0
Cost of entry will be a barrier to EMR adoption in small and medium-size physician offices	57	36	6	1

product. Much has changed. Today's healthcare technology is almost entirely leveraged on commercial platforms. Advances in desktop computers, laptops, tablets, wireless technology, databases, and even development languages, all previously in the realm of the computer hobbyist, have led to new possibilities and ideas on which new generations of clinical applications have been created.

The first generation of these tools was impressive, because they worked where others before them had failed. The users of these products were primarily back-office staff and the occasional visionary clinician. As clinical applications have evolved to become point-of-care solutions, the need for intuitive, reliable, and mature technology has become clear.

As advancements in technology continue at a significant pace, they will have a positive impact on the development and maturing of clinical applications. Important advances in wireless technology that allow clinicians to more easily match their natural workflows, the reliability and speed of new-generation computing to match the needs of real-time decision support, and advances in software presentation tools that offer intuitive end-user interfaces are among a few of the immediate benefits on the horizon that will accelerate EMR usage. More than nine out of ten *Futurescan* survey respondents believe that continued advancements in technology will be key drivers of EMR adoption.

Quality and Outcome Measures

Healthcare organizations are being asked to provide more and more information on a wider array of services to an expanding list of groups. The Joint Commission on Accreditation of Healthcare Organizations, the Centers for Medicare and Medicaid Services, the Institute for Healthcare Improvement, and the American Heart Association, to name a few, continue to drive new reporting standards that are growing in their complexity. In light of the ever-expanding amount of data to be collected and externally reported on, organizations must be positioned to provide the necessary information not only accurately, but also efficiently.

The assumption is that these reporting requirements, none overwhelming on their own but substantial as a whole, will continue to drive the use of EMRs. Although it is not clear that this trend will drive adoption by choice, the understanding is emerging that there is probably no other way to collect the information efficiently and rapidly.

The concept of the EMR producing quality and outcome information as a byproduct of clinical documentation has long been around. The benefits of EMRs as a way to drive quality by mining rich repositories of data to support clinical improvement efforts were some of the earliest wins on which many healthcare IT projects were sold. Although these core benefits of data collection will continue, the newer twist is the rise of pay-for-performance criteria and other similar measures that are beginning to change the paradigm of healthcare financing by linking quality and payment. In this framework, the case for the EMR becomes stronger as it extends beyond the quality realm into the financial one. Eighty-six percent of *Futurescan* survey respondents believe that quality and outcome measures, including new payer reporting requirements, will be key drivers of EMR adoption.

Interoperability and Standards

Interoperability in healthcare is loosely defined as the concept of sharing clinical data among providers from diverse entities. Standards are seen as the necessary precursor to any meaningful sharing. The irony, however, is that advancements are needed intraorganizationally before major progress can be made interorganizationally. Fortunately, as it turns out, solving one problem facilitates a solution to the other.

The challenge in achieving data sharing based on standards is related to the maturity model outlined above. Historically, as IT has evolved in other industries, products migrate from purely proprietary solutions to open-model standards. The challenge with health IT systems is that although that movement has begun, the landscape is still largely characterized by many niche players developing specialized applications. This specialization tends to lend itself to customization, which is rarely the friend of standards.

As EMRs continue to evolve, two major trends are likely. The first is more rapid consolidation in the number of players. The second is a movement away from data as a resource that is sold and managed by vendors to data as a commodity that is owned by the institution or group using the product. Within this framework, the question then becomes, what can act to accelerate this movement?

This is the potential role for state or federal governments and the rapidly proliferating private or public entities known as RHIOs (regional health information organizations). The recent entry of the federal government into standards development—first, as the largest purchaser of IT in the country, second, as a regulator, and finally, as the occupant of the political bully pulpit—has given much-needed momentum to this issue. Although the goal of making information seamlessly available to providers when they need patient data is compelling and the benefits to be gained are promising, the precursor to information sharing—data standards—could have a more immediate impact on accelerating the rate of adoption of EMRs.

The landscape today in EMRs has no common language. Advances in establishing these standards or language will lead to direct improvements in system configuration, improved ease of use for clinicians (through familiarity with terms and concepts), and greater acceptance of out-of-box configurations, leading to fewer required customizations. Two-thirds of *Futurescan* survey respondents agree that federal and state interoperability initiatives will remove barriers and encourage EMR adoption.

Like politics, all healthcare is local. RHIOs, properly structured, can play an important role in facilitating local discussions within and among adjacent communities so that decisions about what is shared are driven by patient and provider need, not by the technology.

Costs and Sponsorship

While the debate continues as to the many reasons healthcare has been slow to adopt IT and whether the players in the field have been resistant to change, the bugaboo of cost will not go away. The price of technology tends to diminish over time, but the opportunities for improvement, waste reduction, and quality enhancement tend to grow equally as an offset, keeping the cost of entry high.

There is a financial barrier to EMR adoption. Three of every four physicians practice in groups of five or fewer (Figure 8), yet EMR adoption lags among such practices, with only one-quarter of physicians in groups of three to five reporting EMR use (Figure 9). With large medical groups and hospitals alike struggling to fund their own major initiatives, it is hard to imagine how a doctor practicing alone in an office will be able to manage the full expense.

Ninety-three percent of *Futurescan* survey respondents believe that cost will be a barrier to EMR adoption in small and medium-size physician offices. Largely for this reason, support is growing for explicit fraud and abuse exceptions to the physician self-referral, antikickback, and civil monetary penalty laws to enable hospitals, medical groups, and others to donate health IT to physicians. Seventy-one percent of *Futurescan* survey respondents agree that removal of such government financial barriers will encourage physicians to adopt the EMR.

Implications for Hospital Leaders

The outlook should be viewed as positive. With technology developments continuing to move forward in a timely way, the clinical quality and payment environment supporting the use of data, standards emerging, and initial rulings on the Stark physician self-referral laws looking favorable, the road ahead for clinical information systems of all types has never looked smoother. Let the hard work begin.

Figure 8. Percentage Distribution of Physicians, by Practice Size

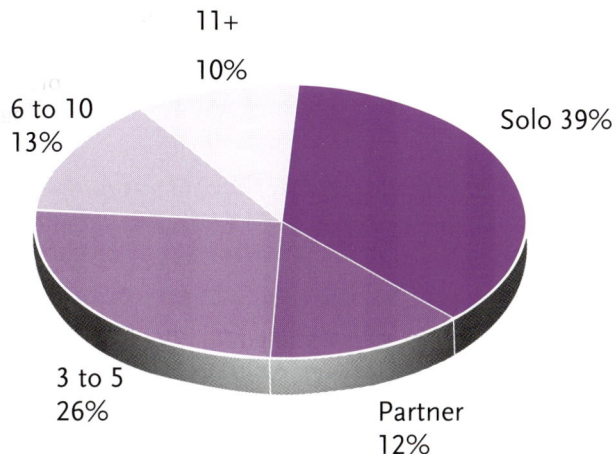

Source: Centers for Disease Control. National Ambulatory Medical Care Survey (NAMCS): Electronic Medical Record Use by Office-Based Physicians, United States, 2005.

Figure 9. Percentage Distribution of Physicians Reporting EMR Use, by Practice Size

Source: Centers for Disease Control. National Ambulatory Medical Care Survey (NAMCS): Electronic Medical Record Use by Office-Based Physicians, United States, 2005.

CONTRIBUTORS

The 2007 edition of *Futurescan* is the latest in a series of environmental assessments for healthcare leaders that the Society for Healthcare Strategy and Market Development has published annually since 1999. It continues the tradition established by the late Russell C. Coile, Jr., who originated *Futurescan* and was its sole author until his death in 2003.

Society for Healthcare Strategy and Market Development
Executive editor: Don Seymour
Board of directors: Susan M. Alcorn (2006 president), Mark Parrington, Joyce M. Ross
Executive director: Lauren A. Barnett
Managing editor: Karen W. Porter

American College of Healthcare Executives/Health Administration Press
Executive vice president/COO: Deborah J. Bowen, FACHE, CAE
Survey administration and tabulation: Peter A. Weil, Ph.D., FACHE, and Peter Kimball
Director, Health Administration Press: Maureen C. Glass, FACHE, CAE
Project manager: Helen-Joy Lynerd, CAE
Layout editor and cover design: Chris Underdown

The Society for Healthcare Strategy and Market Development is the premier organization for healthcare planners, marketers, and communications and public relations professionals. A personal membership group of the American Hospital Association, SHSMD serves more than 4,400 members and is the largest organization in the nation devoted to serving the needs of healthcare strategy professionals. The Society is committed to helping its members meet the future with more knowledge and opportunity as their organizations work to improve health status and quality of life in their communities. For more information, visit SHSMD's website at www.shsmd.org.

The American College of Healthcare Executives is an international professional society of 30,000 healthcare executives who lead hospitals, healthcare systems, and other healthcare organizations. ACHE is known for its prestigious credentialing and educational programs and its Annual Congress on Healthcare Leadership. ACHE's publishing division, Health Administration Press, is one of the largest publishers of books and journals on all aspects of health services management. For more information, visit ACHE's website at www.ache.org.

Leadership Presentations Available
Executive editor Don Seymour is available for on-site leadership presentations to healthcare governing boards, senior management, and medical staffs. To arrange for a leadership presentation, contact Mr. Seymour (617.462.4313 or don@donseymourassociates.com) or the Society for Healthcare Strategy and Market Development (312.422.3743 or shsmd@aha.org).

ABOUT THE SPONSORS

Solucient®, a Thomson business, is an information products company serving the healthcare industry. It is the market leader in providing tools and vital insights that healthcare managers use to improve the performance of their organizations. By integrating, standardizing, and enhancing healthcare information, Solucient provides comparative measurements of cost, quality, and market performance.

VHA Inc., based in Irving, Texas, is a national alliance that provides industry-leading supply chain management services and supports the formation of regional and national networks to help members improve their clinical and economic performance. With 17 offices across the United States, VHA has a track record of proven results in serving more than 2,400 healthcare organizations nationwide.

ABOUT THE *FUTURESCAN* NATIONAL SURVEY

The *Futurescan* National Survey asked 1,600 CEO members of the American College of Healthcare Executives and 2,944 provider-based members of the Society for Healthcare Strategy and Market Development with the title of manager or higher their opinions as to the likelihood of various trends occurring on a widespread basis by 2012. A total of 1,666 responses were received—801 from ACHE-affiliated hospital CEOs and 865 from SHSMD members—for a combined response rate of 37 percent.